THE APPROPRIA

form

To Ernest

THE
APPROPRIATE
FORM

An Essay on the Novel

by

BARBARA HARDY

'No great work of art
dare want its appropriate form'
S. T. Coleridge

Northwestern University Press
1971

PN
3335
H3
1971

ACKNOWLEDGEMENTS

CHAPTER Four originally appeared in *Essays in Criticism*, and I am grateful to the editors for permitting me to reprint it here.

My debts to other critics, colleagues, students, and friends are many and various but I should like to express particular gratitude to the people who have read and criticized parts of the book in manuscript: to my husband, to Jerome Beaty, to Graham Handley, W. J. Harvey, and Reginald Levy. I am grateful too to the adviser of the Athlone Press from whose comments I have profited. My special thanks are due to Martin Dodsworth who undertook to look up certain details in the Russian text of *Anna Karenina*, and whose researches so strengthened and extended my own analysis that they are printed as an appendix to Chapter VII.

B.H.

CONTENTS

Introduction   1

I.   Total Relevance: Henry James   11

II.   The Matter and the Treatment: Henry James   30

III.   Dogmatic Form: Daniel Defoe, Charlotte Brontë, Thomas Hardy, and E. M. Forster   51

IV.   The Structure of Imagery: George Meredith's *Harry Richmond*   83

V.   Implication and Incompleteness: George Eliot's *Middlemarch*   105

VI.   Truthfulness and Schematism: D. H. Lawrence   132

VII.   Form and Freedom: Tolstoy's *Anna Karenina*   174

Appendix: A Note on Certain Revisions in *Anna Karenina*   212

Index   217

Introduction

My subject is the variety of narrative form, illustrated by a sample of a few novels and novelists sufficiently representative and distinctive.[1] Before enlarging on individuality and difference, it seems useful to begin with some brief and obvious remarks about the basic kinds of organization in fiction. The novelist, whoever he is and whenever he is writing, is giving form to a story, giving form to his moral and metaphysical views, and giving form to his particular experience of sensations, people, places, and society.

He tells a story. Even in the recent French anti-novel, this entails clarity, continuity, and a rising curve of expectation. The action of the story may be minimal, as it is in *The Square*, by Marguerite Duras, or dislocated, as it is in Alain Robbe-Grillet, or muted and attenuated, as it is in Virginia Woolf. It may be violent and exciting, as it is in Dickens and Graham Greene, or depend less on external adventure than on the troubled consciousness and feelings, as it does in D. H. Lawrence's *Women in Love*. It may be the chief principle of organization, as it is in *Wuthering Heights* or *Jane Eyre*, where the actual physical events provide the primary means of delineating character and change, or it may provide a fitfully recurring tension as it does in Dickens,

[1] I should draw attention, perhaps unnecessarily, to the limits of my selected novels and novelists. I have said nothing about the symbolic novels of such writers as Kafka or Camus, where my criterion of truthfulness seems to apply only in a very special sense, since in these novels the immediacy and individual identity is frankly subdued to the structure of fable, and realistic surface is abrogated. Symbolic fable can reveal human truths with a special intensity and power, but my concern has been with fiction attempting, at least in part, some degree of psychological realism. D. H. Lawrence's *Women in Love* might be regarded as a symbolic fable but appears to me to be a mixed form, possessing the realism of psychological detail and individual identity.

where the story line does not always coincide with moral criticism or social satire.   It may be placed in the context of long spaces of routine or randomly flowing experience, as it is in *Anna Karenina*. It may be very simple, as in Jane Austen, or highly complicated, as in George Eliot. But if the novel does not possess the form of the story then it is not a novel.

Even defiant story-tellers like Sterne or Joyce or Robbe-Grillet have either had to retain its rudimentary features or have had to exploit the very form they were flouting. *Tristram Shandy* tantalizes conventional narrative expectations but only succeeds in its teasing satire by keeping within the limits of fiction and occasionally satisfying our need to know what happened next. We may often be told what happened before instead of what happened afterwards, we may never know what happened in the end, but the whole ingenious structure is committed to the form of expectation and curiosity.

In telling his story, or in between telling his story, the novelist is also organizing his criticism of life. He may be fitting the complexity and contradictoriness of life into a predetermined dogmatic pattern, like Defoe and Charlotte Brontë or Hardy. He may be using dogmatic patterns in order to test and reject them, like George Eliot and Tolstoy and Lawrence. He may be less interested in showing ideals and models than in rejecting them, but, like the story, the moral view is always present in some form or another even in crude stereotyped novels. Its form is the form of moral categories, which the novel shares with the psychologist's case-book or with almost anyone's gossip, but although the unity of moral category is a very important aspect of the form of a novel, it is not the aspect which defines its peculiar qualities as a novel. In order to be a novel, and not an abstract analysis, it must give substance to individuality as well as to categories.

The novel holds us by its story and informs us by its

moral argument, but it moves us by its individual presences and moments, by what Lawrence calls 'the living moment' and 'the vivid relation . . . at that quick moment of time' and by what James calls 'the love of each seized identity.' This kind of separation of morality and truthful realization is arbitrary, since the novelist's evaluation of life is worked out in particular, not in general, terms. A moral scheme can be made to seem workable, a metaphysical argument plausible, by an art which leaves out the individual stubbornness of facts and feelings. For this reason I have avoided the word 'realism' and fallen back on 'truthfulness'. As Robert Louis Stevenson said of 'truth',[1] this is a term 'of debatable propriety' but useful since it is suggestive both of a satisfactory translation of experience into art and of an honest and sensitive recognition of facts and feelings often evaded and avoided in life, not merely in art. If the concept of form is to be used faithfully and usefully it must be enlarged to include the individual life which is the breath of fiction and of a real response to fiction. And this real response is much more than a recognition of our familiar experience, must often involve that new recognition which, as Lawrence knew, was frequently painful. Telling the truth in fiction is not invariably different from telling the truth in life, though our response to a novel involves both the comparison with the world we know and the new apprehension of the world we do not know.

It may be objected at this point that I am emptying all meaning from the term 'form'. I hope that the detailed argument in the body of the book will succeed in demonstrating that we can enlarge the scope of the term without such a loss. The truthful detail may look irrelevant if we see form in a merely skeletal way, as the form of the story or the form of moral categories. If we look also for the form of particularity I think we can do justice to the difficulty and power of the novelist's art and stay honestly close to the

[1] See p. 32.

reader's response. If we admire the narrative curve of
tension we may place Trollope higher than Tolstoy. If we
admire the thematic organization we may place James
Gould Cozzens higher than Lawrence. If we admire the
form of truth, we can do neither.

These three aspects of the art of fiction may be all strongly
present, as they are in *Great Expectations* and *Middlemarch*,
two novels remarkable for their harmonious combination of
the good story, the working-out of a moral problem, and the
lively representation of reality. Not all critics and novelists
would admit these novels as ideal forms. I would myself
argue that the form of represented truth in *Middlemarch* is
not perfect, and that this has often been ignored, or ack-
nowledged but not expressed as formal criticism, because
critics have been more interested in the novel's narrative
and moral organization than in the completeness and
consistency of its imitation of life. This is using formal
analysis and formal criteria in a very wide sense, one very
unlike the analysis and criteria of our first great critic of
fiction, Henry James. James also denied formal harmony
to such great Victorians as Dickens and George Eliot, but
granted their life while he denied their art. He would
certainly not have admitted my suggested three purposes of
fiction, since they include no mention of form for its own
sake. James did more than anyone to define the aesthetic
status of fiction, and it seems apparent from his various
discussions of narrative form, that he became more interested
in giving the novel a strong and conspicuous aesthetic
interest than in telling a good story, or working out a moral
argument, or making a representation of life as it feels when
we live it. He did all these things, usually did them sup-
remely well, and was by no means unaware of their existence
and importance, as is vividly apparent in his tribute to
Balzac's 'insistent particulars' and 'love of each seized
identity' ('The Lesson of Balzac', *The House of Fiction*,
ed. Leon Edel). But he was chiefly concerned with

praising and publicizing a conspicuously aesthetic and intensely concentrated form. Both in his novels and in his rejection of the large loose baggy monsters of the mid-nineteenth century we find the aesthetic principle which is left out in my division of narrative form into the story, the argument, and the imitation of life. James could not deny that those novelists he attacked gave form to a story or to a criticism of life or to psychological experience, but what he could and did find lacking was his own kind of narrative form. This is the form of a highly concentrated unity, the result of the rigid economy which is essential in drama and possible, though rare, in fiction. Looked at another way, it is an assertive display of form which is common in music and the plastic arts, and rare in fiction.

James saw himself as refining and toughening the forms of fiction, and not merely in a way appropriate for himself, a choice from many possible experiments in the medium. He saw this as the best way. Nor indeed did he see his experiment as intrinsically fraught with dangers and limitations, and this is not really surprising. His remarkable achievement is the creation of a narrowly limited and even gratuitously stringent form, which only rarely distorts his human materials. The last thing I want to do is to applaud the expansive realism of George Eliot and Tolstoy by presenting James as the model of aesthetic form and a typically damaging instance of its falsity. We can, I suggest, recognize both his triumph and the triumph of George Eliot and Tolstoy if we admit that there are intrinsic difficulties and dangers in the aesthetic assertion and concentration. To take note of the failures in James is to equip ourselves for recognizing his successes. He himself accused George Eliot not only of 'redundancy' but also of sacrificing 'the irresponsible plastic way' to her intellectual system ('The Life of George Eliot', *Partial Portraits*). His aesthetic ideal also took its toll. If we recognize, for instance, that the concluding rejection of Maria Gostrey at the end of *The Ambassadors* makes an affirmation which is thematically and aesthetically satisfactory but humanly rather unsupported, we can better appreciate the reasons why the end of *The Wings of the Dove* is both formally essential and very moving. Once we appreciate the difficulties involved in the Jamesian dramatic economy we come to see his reasons for flouting the author's voice as used by George Eliot. George Eliot's commentary has form and function, but when James keeps rigidly within the consciousness of Strether he is surely achieving something impossible within the looser form of the conventional Victorian novel. We should add that George Eliot achieves effects which James does not, but what is important is the individual achievement, not the competition between narrative forms.

James's formal stringency is not the only source of assertive order and selected pattern. The dogmatist has his schematism too, and in some of the novels of Defoe and Charlotte Brontë and Hardy we find another kind of concentrated form, much less aesthetically conspicuous than anything in James but also very different from the expansive qualifications of George Eliot and Tolstoy. If James is on occasion guilty of sacrificing human plausibility to economy and symmetry, Defoe and Hardy are more frequently guilty of sacrificing the exception or the qualification which would blur what seems to them to be the typical pattern in life. Here of course we are on notably different ground, since the ideological simplification or distortion is not just a literary imitation, to be judged as realistic or unrealistic. It is an error or a partiality or a blindness or a fantasy which may be transferred from life to art. Both aesthetic selection and dogmatic selection have their dangers and limitations, but both can yield vitality enough to make a novel which is more than either a pleasing form or a plain fable, and which has the colour of life.

I have tried to show the limitations of form in novels

which generally contrive to overcome them in an imaginative apprehension of truth. James achieved vitality under hard conditions, just as George Eliot achieved unity while exploring the widest variations and complexities. Tolstoy's *Anna Karenina* probably comes nearest to a form which preserves unity and meaningful contrast while keeping close to the apparently formless flow of experience. All three, in very different ways, make their individual forms out of what James call the 'awful mixture of things'. I might have enlarged my account of this formal variety by giving other examples of restriction. The novels of Virginia Woolf would provide simpler and cruder examples of the aesthetic novel than anything James ever wrote, while the simple early Victorian Christian novels of Elizabeth Sewell or Charlotte Yonge, often directly designed as instruments of religious education, would be stark instances of the distortions of dogmatic form. But I have not wanted to attempt a large classification, but merely to show the variety of combinations in novelists for whom I have strong sympathy and admiration.

I would not want to disguise my belief that the expansive novel has its special advantages. The Tolstoyan form has a richness and freedom and immediacy peculiar to itself, and this is not always sufficiently recognized even by critics who are fervent in their rejection of James's partiality. We have by now accepted the deficiencies of James as a judge of other novelists, but what seems to have happened is that we still use the Jamesian formal standards with little qualification in our own analysis. We insist that the large loose baggy monster has unity, has symbolic concentration, has patterns of imagery and a thematic construction of character, and in the result the baggy monster is processed by our New Criticism into something strikingly like the original Jamesian streamlined beast. In attacking James for passing an act of uniformity against the novelists we seem to be in danger of still pressing his standards of uniformity, not claiming that Tolstoy and James are achieving different kinds of imaginative form, but at least appearing to claim that the novels James rejected were other versions of his own achievement. This is, I believe, to belittle and blur the individual power of James and Tolstoy and George Eliot. I have tried to show that there is after all some sense in calling novels like *Middlemarch* and *Anna Karenina* large and loose, but that this largeness and looseness has a special advantage, allowing the novelist to report truthfully and fully the quality of the individual moment, the loose end, the doubt and contradiction and mutability. James was wrong to call such novels 'fluid puddings' but we might do worse than keep his adjective while rejecting his noun.

We can only bracket George Eliot and Tolstoy for temporary convenience of contrast. If George Eliot makes Hardy and James at times appear thinly schematic, so in turn does Tolstoy make George Eliot at times appear over-optimistic and final in her moral analysis, and restricted in her report of life. *Middlemarch* is very like *Anna Karenina* in its ability to create and break categories, and in its truth to the complexity and shifts of human emotion, but it has a pattern of moral development and conclusiveness which Tolstoy blurs in truthful doubt. It has too a conventional exclusion of sex which is very visible if we put it beside *Anna Karenina* or *Lady Chatterley's Lover*, two novels which I want to bracket only temporarily in contrast with *Middlemarch*, since sexual realism is by no means the same thing in Tolstoy and Lawrence. But if we are considering the truthfulness of the large expansive novel we should bear in mind that social convention imposed a restriction on George Eliot just as surely as self-imposed artistic discipline imposed restrictions on James. The limitation of E. M. Forster's disarmingly argued suggestion that we can look at novelists as if they were working together in a circular room is that it ignores those historical conditions which determine form as well as theme. George Eliot and Lawrence are plainly not working in the same room, and although they are both remarkably honest novelists, the limitations of Forster's metaphor are clearly apparent if we put *Middlemarch* beside *Lady Chatterley's Lover*.

Lawrence throws into sharp relief not only those evasions and omissions which we take for granted in the Victorian novel, but is, like Tolstoy, a good example of the novelist whose form is closely conditioned by the conscious relation of his art to his life. Lawrence is the most complete antithesis to James, for he rejects external formal principles, demands the right to make the novel reflect the illogicality, absurdity, and intransigence of life, eschews finality, and usually defies the diagrammatic forms of fable. But we can only use critical comparison if we, like the truthful novelist, give up the neatness of categories when they cease to correspond to the richness of our material. In some ways Lawrence resembles James: his symbolic unity, his psychic converse between characters, and his frequently concentrated point of view, all force the critic to modify the antithesis. Moreover, if we compare Lawrence with George Eliot and Tolstoy, he shows occasional lapses into that very schematism he attacks most fiercely in theory. If *Lady Chatterley's Lover* is more complete in its sexual frankness than *Middlemarch*, it has the disadvantage of a serious lapse into schematic fable which makes Sir Clifford Chatterley an implausible construct compared with the lovingly rendered Casaubon. It will not do to suggest that Lawrence is free to tell the whole truth because he is unaesthetic compared with James, undogmatic compared with Hardy, and socially uninhibited compared with George Eliot. Some of the factors which determine form can be isolated, but not all, and if Lawrence has the explicable advantages of his chosen form he also shows less explicable failures and inconsistencies.

One of my chief interests in this comparison of novels and novelists is the relation between generalization and particular liveliness, and, as I have just suggested, the critic must keep an eye on his categories, useful though they are up to a point. Up to a point it is possible to define some of the variations of narrative form by erecting a scaffolding of categories. We can suggest that some novels are externally and internally more restricted than others, some expressing a fixed opinion in a fixed pattern, some coming to value means as much as ends, some deferring pragmatically to the confusion and relativity of judgement and solution. Such a scaffolding is only useful if it is admittedly impermanent, and it is no use throwing in such an admission at the beginning and end of discussion. I have tried to modify my classification wherever it seem to be becoming misleading, and this may at times have resulted in a tiresome process of shifting contrast and comparison. The novel shows us the artist and moralist who is prepared to disprove, not only to prove, his hypotheses, though at times it is hard to say whether he is open-eyed or unaware when he blurs conclusion or goes against the grain of his own beliefs. If we are to attempt any celebration and analysis of the most various and least aesthetic moral art—the art of fiction—we must use our categories as probes rather than proofs. If the differences I describe in my chosen novelists turn out to be less impressive than the common features, it would be unreasonable of me to object.

CHAPTER I

Total Relevance: Henry James

HENRY JAMES is almost always telling a single story, while Dickens and George Eliot and Tolstoy are telling several. This simple difference of scope and quantity determines many differences of form, and should not be neglected, though it is by no means the most interesting difference between James's concentrated narrative and the expansive novels of the great Victorians. What distinguishes the Jamesian novel from its large loose baggy contemporaries is the special relation of its parts to the whole. It would take too much space to examine fully all the characteristics of the Jamesian economy, and my purpose here is to choose some of those features which have not already been exhaustively discussed in order to bring out some of the merits and defects which make him significantly different from most other novelists. A full account would have to include discussion of his symbolism, his dramatic prefiguration, his allusiveness, and his irony. I have left out some of these subjects entirely, and only briefly touched on others. For similar reasons, I have not treated his novels chronologically, though I am aware that his formal concentration varies and develops. Nor have I treated the novels very evenly. After a lengthy discussion of some of the formal problems of the late novels, I have thrown out some barely substantiated remarks on similar problems elsewhere. If this makes some of my judgements appear flimsy, I can only plead that I wanted to keep James in his place in this book, as an illustration in danger of swallowing my thesis, but I hope not actually doing so.

George Eliot expressed the hope that every detail in *Middlemarch* had its place in the total design. *Middlemarch* is indeed a novel with no irrelevant digressions, no disturbing loose ends, no padding either of humour or circumstantial description or local colour. It is not, however, a novel where every episode, every description, every psychological observation, and every metaphor, is of equal importance. Its total design is that of an intricately graduated order. Some details are more important than others, some of its most vivid and memorable moments lie apart from the main action and the main moral argument. They may well command a powerful assent of feeling or thought, they often suggest the pressure and possibility of actions and choices not taken up within the novel, and in these and other ways they have their part to play in building up the substantial appearance of truth. Some of the details could be dropped without much loss to the main figure in the carpet. The development of Dorothea's story, in all its moral and psychological implication, could not do without Will Ladislaw's relationship with Rosamond Vincy, which precipitates a crisis, change, and conclusion. But it could do without the striking moment when Ladislaw sees, as a distinct possibility, that he may be undesiringly led into adultery with Rosamond. This single realistic flash of vision—hardly ever mentioned by George Eliot's critics—is a local truth, not an essential detail in the argument. The fact that we are never told why the railwayman in *Anna Karenina* was killed—he may have been drunk or too muffled against the cold to hear the train—in no way affects the action or the major ironies and symbols, but its local effect of casualness and ignorance has its part to play in the complete truthfulness of the novel. We should accept Bartle Massey's crusty bachelor dislike of women in *Adam Bede* without the hints about his past history, but the glimpse, incomplete and brief and unsentimental, gives us that sense of characters acting from a complete existence which is so characteristic of George

Eliot. There is a powerful image used in Chapter xv of *Middlemarch* to express Lydgate's ability to see beyond his passion for Laure while in its grips: 'while we rave on the heights, [we] behold the wide plain where our persistent self pauses and awaits us'. It has no place in the image-patterns of the novel and does not even express one of the dominant themes, but its local reminder of Lydgate's double vision—extended and brought home in the generalization—is deeply moving.

There are many such details in the expansive novel which play a small but cumulatively important part in building up a truthful impression of human complexity. This sounds vague, and I think necessarily so. It is hard to see how the critic can demonstrate the cumulative effect of particular details and moments which cannot be reduced to a poetic or thematic pattern. What is possible is some account of moments of feeling or sensation which are striking even though formally isolated. How often, in our criticism of novels, do we pick out such moving details which may testify to a sensitive if unmethodical response? I do not suggest that criticism should revert to this kind of impressionism, but merely that there is perhaps something wrong with a critical account of a novel which mentions only those details and images which fit into a symbolic series or a codifiable moral argument. If we apply the Jamesian standards of cross-reference and total relevance then we may move too far away from the actual experience of responding to fiction. If our test is strictly thematic or poetic, then we may judge such details as irrelevant or, in James's word, 'arbitrary'. What we often do in practice is to exaggerate the symbolic relevance. We describe those moths which flap round when Karenin discusses his divorce with the lawyer as symbols of Anna's situation, point out that the story of Rumpelstiltskin told by Mary Garth at the Vincys' party is significantly placed in a novel about work, bargains, marriage, and nemesis. What we do equally often is just to forget about such details. The investigation of the wide significance of small points has become standardized. It is a teachable method, and can be applied by almost anyone capable of reading, writing, and counting. But how often do we publish our negative evidence—the images which do not belong to the pattern, the detail which is simply a detail, like *Lovers' Vows* in *Mansfield Park*, which so many of us have read eagerly and found to our disappointment to have no symbolic resonance?

The novel is usually concerned with giving a substantial picture of human relationships, and if this fails no amount of serious purpose or poetic unity can make it a good novel. But the unpopularity of character-analysis in Shakespearean criticism may have made its contribution to our exaggerated emphasis on theme and symbolism. If we content ourselves with doing only what D. H. Lawrence called 'reducing the novel to its didactic capacity' or with regarding the novel as a poem—which it is not—we lose the necessary respect for the insistent local appearances of truth.

The novels of Dickens and George Eliot may be distorted by such analysis, but the novels of Henry James will suffer much less. For the unusual feature of the Jamesian novel—particularly the three late novels—is that it makes it almost impossible for us to maintain such a distinction between local effect and central relevance. The local vividness of person or scene or object is nearly always a symbolic contribution to the main action and argument. The loose detail is seldom found in the clear definition and compressed observation of a Jamesian novel. When James withholds information—as he does of course on several celebrated occasions—his silence is portentous and conspicuous, and echoes throughout the novel. Compare his evasion about Milly's illness or the nature of the small object manufactured by Chad's ancestors with Tolstoy's tiny, quiet, barely noticeable refusal to give a full report on the reasons for the railwayman's death in *Anna Karenina*. The gratuitous detail, or the assertive silence, which need not be the result of careless or imperfect organization, contributes to the lifelike impression of a world which has blurred and imperfectly known details, rough edges, loose ends, and unacted possibilities. This is not the kind of world created by James.

The details which might be gratuitous in another novel, such as the idle flow of talk at a dinner-party or the furniture in a room, or gestures or colours, sooner or later impress us (sooner rather than later) as having a density of reference, a large irony, a symbolic weight, when they make their cunning appearances in *The Portrait of a Lady* or *The Wings of the Dove*. There is no free observation in the concentrated Jamesian novel. The observer himself is never free to be a mere recorder, but is always using the external appearances in order to pick up cues and clues. James gives us a dramatically enclosed and self-contained world where everything has relevance to the main argument, where appearances, gestures, objects, images, conversation, all shoot out like sure arrows to the heart of the matter. His pattern is insistently centripetal, his relevance is total. And its definition is simpler and clearer and has a more immediate aesthetic assertiveness, like the form of a song or a pot, than that of the novel whose intricate structure keeps greater faith with the complexities, uncertainties, and changes of its raw life materials.

On the face of it, the novel dealing with the single action has plenty of chance to be leisurely and wayward, while the three-volume novel has special needs for economy. Dickens and George Eliot have to make many transitions in action, persons, time, place, and atmosphere. They usually have to make a serial construction memorable, coherent, and unified. I am referring here not to serial publication, for this of course applies to James too, but to the serial structure of a multiple novel when read straight off, with the regular interruptions not of time but of its rotating stories. The dense symbolic scenes of Tolstoy and George Eliot show the characteristic economy of the large loose form. There is the first scene in the railway-station in *Anna Karenina*. It is an intricate meeting-place and a beginning, a knot of symbolism and irony in which past, present, and future and three sets of destiny are bound together. There is the scene of Featherstone's funeral in *Middlemarch* where Dorothea looks down reluctantly from the window, and refuses, like her author, to echo Mrs Cadwallader's views on the grotesque humanity seen below. This scene, too, is a strongly symbolic and ironical condensation of time and action and persons. Another source of unity is found in the binding power of recurrent imagery and symbols, especially functional in George Eliot and Dickens. The special need for unity in the large novel is met in various ways, and even in lesser masters of the form, like Trollope or even Harriet Beecher Stowe, the need to cover large tracts of time and place and to handle a variety of people and events makes some modes of economy and tightness essential. The large novel which is also rambling and discrete is by any standards a loose monstrosity, but it is very different from the novels of Dickens, George Eliot, and Tolstoy.

It would be an exaggeration to suggest that this kind of condensation is sustained throughout the great Victorian long novel. For one pregnant scene of the kind I have mentioned, there are many which have slighter general reference, like some of the domestic scenes in *Middlemarch* or the comic scenes in Dickens, where it would be hard to argue the pressure of total relevance. There are many scenes in the expansive novel which have the uncommitted air of life's normal flow, standing outside crisis and symbolic vividness, sketching in social manners and connections and familiarizing rather than developing character, and providing the necessary illusion of a slow movement of time and a natural unfolding of character and action. There is a special kind of leisureliness associated with *Middlemarch* and *Anna*

Karenina, though they are not chronicle novels like *David Copperfield* or *The Mill on the Floss* or *War and Peace*, but have a much briefer time-span. This leisureliness is one of the results of the novelist's ability to suggest the ordinary life between crises. Tolstoy, in particular, has a remarkable capacity for filling the novel with scenes which lie right outside the tensions of plot, corresponding most closely with the normal pace of life, not shaped by the climactic curves leading to crises and conclusions.

In the late novels of James, and indeed in most of his early work too, each scene vibrates with the expectancy leading to the crisis, and a remarkable number of scenes are actual scenes of crisis, either of consciousness or event. Each scene has the resonance and totally committed relevance of the railway-station scene in *Anna Karenina* or the funeral scene in *Middlemarch*. James's interest in the theatre, his own experiments in drama, and his insistent use of dramatic analogy in his remarks on the novel, serve as reminders that this kind of condensation of scene and symbol is something we find more often in the drama than in fiction. Characteristic of drama too, and another source of condensation in James, is the absence of the narrator, except in a very muted form. Every detail has to tell in the dramatic medium, and James uses details as Humpty-Dumpty uses words, making them work overtime. For the novel does not demand this kind of insistent condensation. It is not restricted in time, like a play. All its parts are accessible: we can always turn back its pages. James's extra demands may have been necessary to him, but they are not the necessary responses to the exigencies of his medium. Since I am claiming total relevance for James I cannot provide effective illustration, and my claim will be meaningless unless every reader checks for himself throughout the course of the novel. But in an attempt to illustrate I shall look at some scenes from *The Wings of the Dove*, not scenes of crisis in the ordinary sense of the word, but typical examples of James's insistent central relevance. In the dialogue and in the visual particulars there is a depth of irony which does not blur or distance the actual scene, but which takes us beyond that scene. The phenomenal world never shines innocently in its own right in James, but it is not reduced or schematized out of existence. One of the most interesting qualities of his insistent condensation is his ability to give the symbol without losing vital particularity.

In Chapter vii of *The Wings of the Dove* Lord Mark and Milly Theale are sitting next to each other at dinner, and James gives us a conversation with the appropriate surface of wit, flattery, and exaggeration. Such remarks as 'You're the best thing now' and 'you shall see everything' have perfect propriety and verisimilitude for the people and the social occasion. But James also ensures that the superficial appearance of small-talk shall vibrate portentously, shall strike us as small-talk with a difference. He manages this in several ways. First, by a favourite device of his which he uses in several novels, and which is to be found in a much cruder form in *Daniel Deronda*, at the first meeting of Grandcourt and Gwendolen. This is the device of unspoken dialogue. After Lord Mark tells Milly that she 'shall see everything' the dialogue is suspended while we move into Milly's unspoken reflections. Hers is a consciousness both febrile and acute, marked by feelings of isolation, unreality, and by an obsession which makes her most plausibly read this stranger's polite remarks as *double-entendres*. Lord Mark's actual words are sufficiently pointed to encourage her ironical interpretations, since he is endowed with Jamesian extra-sensory perception, but they are not so pointed that we cannot take them at their face-value. But what he says in the imaginary continuation of their dialogue within Milly's mind cannot be taken at face-value alone. The gap between his small-talk and her larger obsessed interpretation is bridged by what she imagines. This is Milly reading between his lines:

Inexpressive, but intensely significant, he met as no one else could
have done the very question she had suddenly put to Mrs. Stringham
on the Brünig. Should she have it, whatever she did have, that question had been, for long? 'Ah, so possibly not', her neighbour appeared
to reply; 'therefore, don't you see? *I'm* the way.' It was vivid that he
might be, in spite of his absence of flourish; the way being doubtless
just in that absence. (ch. vii)

There is no longer the nice balance between a plausible
social dialogue and an ironical cue for the knowing reader.
Milly's interpretation and extension of Lord Mark's words
does not belong to the context of normal social exchange.
The literal application of 'you shall see everything' is just
not present in '*I'm* the way'. Lord Mark could not know
that she is ill, could not understand her unspoken question
even if he heard it, could not yet be offering himself as
'the way'.

The scene establishes Milly's sick susceptibilities but it
does more than this. It also looks ahead, prefiguring Lord
Mark's later understanding and proposals, though incompletely. Such concentration has a further convenience,
for it establishes that genuine and characteristic *rapport* so
rapidly experienced by many Jamesian characters. These
characters do not need to go through a lengthy process of
getting acquainted. Their endowment of sensibility and
intelligence is exploited by James to bring about this kind
of subterranean, almost telepathic contact. The nearest
thing to this in the novel is Lawrence's psycho-physical
affinities, different in many ways but having some of the
same consequences. James does not use this *rapport* in sexual
relations alone. Indeed, it is usually more marked in asexual
relations, though the contact between Lord Mark and Milly
is an interesting borderline case. Where other novelists may
use the fact or the convention of love at first sight James
exploits the intelligence and sensibility of his people and
creates the convention of speedy *rapport*, which enables him
to leave out many steps and explanations which slow up

and—from a Jamesian point of view—'waste' time in *Middlemarch* and *Anna Karenina*. Both George Eliot and Tolstoy use the sudden *rapport* of sexual tension in the first encounters of Stephen and Maggie, Vronsky and Anna, but only in these fairly restricted amorous situations. The speed with which characters come to understand each other in a Jamesian novel is one of the features of his concentration.

In this example there is both a subjective rendering of events and words and the sense of the ordinary social occasion, though if we follow the movement of the scene it can be seen to move away from the sense of things as they are outside the distorting imagination and stay within Milly's mind. But James does not need the dramatically decorous excuse of sick distortion to achieve this effect. Later in the novel, for instance, he brings about foreshortening and moving brevity by the use of Susan Shepherd Stringham's intuitive knowledge of Lord Mark's interview with Milly. Intuition is exaggerated into telepathic communication between all kinds of people and in all kinds of circumstance, and any account of James's experiments in point of view needs to emphasize this remarkable shortcut.

I am here concerned with the concentration of which the intuitional convention is only one aspect. The casual conversation—or what would be casual conversation in most other novels—is compressed and speeded up, but so too is the presentation of the visible presences of people and objects.

Earlier in this same chapter we are made aware of the room and people not as solid real appearances but as the notation of Milly's consciousness:

The smallest things, the faces, the hands, the jewels of the women, the sound of words, especially of names, across the table, the shape of the forks, the arrangement of the flowers, the attitude of the servants, the walls of the room, were all touches in a picture and denotements in a play; and they marked for her, moreover, her alertness of vision.

Milly's sharpened and uncomfortable consciousness is the point of view, and the world which she observes is not only coloured by her sensibility and predicament but self-consciously and intelligently interpreted by her. She sees her own unnaturally sharpened vision. The dramatic correlative is to be found in many forms in many novels but never quite like this. George Eliot observes the deadened appearances of objects to the disenchanted eye, but it is she who observes the distortion, and Maggie or Dorothea respond without recording any awareness of their acts of distortion. Defoe marks the terrified flight of Moll Flanders after she has been tempted to kill a child by giving a long list of street-names, but this is the author's interpolation, conveying the emotion without comment by a symbol standing between the character and the reader. Robbe-Grillet enumerates the appearances of many things in *Jealousy* to convey the meticulous and obsessed searching of the jealous eye, but this too is an *objective* correlative. James makes the characters self-consciously formulate the symbolic and personal distortion and this has the special dramatic effect of making the visible world especially relevant while indicating its actual undifferentiated status. Milly moves and observes in a world of solid objects but for her they are transparent, revealing always her plight, her passion for life and her awareness of death. She is made fully aware of her obsessed act of selection. The author is able to stand aside, letting the character 'dramatize', never having to murmur 'poor child, it was not like this at all' in the way George Eliot murmurs her compassionate and ironical wisdom while Caterina wanders through the bright morning, or Hetty Sorrel through the harvest-fields, while Maggie pushes back her hair and eagerly reads on in Thomas à Kempis. The awareness of the characters in James extends beyond an interpretation of the world to a critical awareness of the act of interpretation, and this is again a mode of condensation. And the self-consciousness of this kind of interpretation does not reduce the vitality of the solid world but indeed allows for its existence. The phenomenal world is being interpreted and stands alive outside the self-conscious act.

In Chapter xiii of *The Wings of the Dove* there is condensation through character which is a clearer instance of the combination of symbol and substance. Milly is wandering through the London streets. She has been instructed 'to live' by Sir Luke, whose blend of familiar medical evasiveness and Jamesian cryptic knowingness is brilliantly brought off. Streets, scenes, and people are described in some detail. The objects carry the force of personal relevance as they are interpreted by Milly. Everything in the scene, down to the bench she sits on, is transmitted to us as she sees it and as she sees herself seeing it:

> She had come out, as she presently saw, at the Regent's Park, round which, on two or three occasions with Kate Croy, her public chariot had solemnly rolled. But she went into it further now; this was the real thing; the real thing was to be quite away from the pompous roads, well within the centre and on the stretches of shabby grass. Here were benches and smutty sheep; here were idle lads at games of ball, with their cries mild in the thick air; here were wanderers, anxious and tired like herself; here doubtless were hundreds of others just in the same box. Their box, their great common anxiety, what was it, in this grim breathing-space, but the practical question of life? They could live if they would; that is, like herself, they had been told so; she saw them all about her, on seats, digesting the information, feeling it altered, assimilated, recognising it again as something, in a slightly different shape, familiar enough, the blessed old truth that they would live if they could. All she thus shared with them made her wish to sit in their company; which she so far did that she looked for a bench that was empty, eschewing a still emptier chair that she saw hard by and for which she would have paid, with superiority, a fee.

The pathos and hard truth of this moment belong to a convention older than the novel. This is Milly accepting the classlessness of death. James gives to the irony his own special twist for what is real death for Milly is equated with the poverty of ordinary life around her. The equation is established by a mode of concentrated reference rather like the loaded dialogue of the dinner-party. Here the simple cliché and dead metaphor is given revived precise reference: 'she went into it further now', 'the same box', 'the question of life' and 'breathing-space' point both to Milly and the life around her, and the duplicity of these puns enables her to express, even to work out, her pity for the others and her pity for herself. The scene is full of Milly's sick obsession, but it is also full of meticulous reasoning. The obsession, like Lear's, embraces the general plight, involving an act of compassionate generalization and an insight which is not merely inturned.

Her reflections on the significance of the doctor's response run throughout the Regent's Park scene. Her compassion for the people around is related to his compassion for her:

He dressed out for her the compassion he so signally permitted himself to waste; but its operation for herself was as directly divesting, denuding, exposing. It reduced her to her ultimate state, which was that of a poor girl—with her rent to pay for example—staring before her in a great city. Milly had her rent to pay, her rent for her future; everything else but how to meet it fell away from her in pieces, in tatters. This was the sensation the great man had doubtless not purposed. Well, she must go home, like the poor girl, and see. There might after all be ways; the poor girl too would be thinking. It came back for that matter perhaps to views already presented. She looked about her again, on her feet, at her scattered, melancholy comrades— some of them so melancholy as to be down on their stomachs in the grass, turned away, ignoring, burrowing; she saw once more, with them, those two faces of the question between which there was so little to choose for inspiration. It was perhaps superficially more striking that one could live if one would; but it was more appealing, insinuating, irresistible, in short, that one would live if one could.

Milly converts the world of the park, like the scene at the dinner-party, into a subjective and transparent world of appropriate appearances, metaphors for her predicament which are not mere rhetorical identifications, conceited and convenient, but the literal identifications of genuine sympathy. Her poor neighbours supply the right term only by being seen and felt for what they are. Our impression of her sympathy co-exists with the impression of her reduction to poverty and anxiety and isolation, and, finally, with the impression of the courage which makes her stand up instead of burrowing and turning away. This courage is both a quality to be asserted and a quality to be broken. She is later most literally to become the poor girl because of her poverty and because of her riches. She too is eventually to turn away and burrow like her scattered melancholy comrades.

Here the condensation of scene and sensation answers exactly to James's dictum in *The Art of Fiction*: 'What is character but the determination of incident? What is incident but the illustration of character?' It is largely achieved by conscious symbolic interpretation on the part of the character. Hardy selects the rich and barren land for Tess but it is Milly whose pity and self-pity is made to select the park as her image. We are given not only the external image, filled with irony, but the implications of the despair and love and courage with which she courts anonymity, recognizes anxiety, and defines the question of living and dying. The very explicit act of selection allows full and concrete status to the environment and its people—these are real people and a real grim breathing-space. We discriminate between her self-involvement and the pressure of the real hard world outside because there is no distortion and no sentimentality. The very flaunting of the act of interpretation admits, within the novel, that there is a gap between the world outside and the use she makes of it in formulating her plight. The result of this extremely sophisticated use of pathetic fallacy and imagery is to admit the fallacy and the residual facts beyond it, in a way which the conventional uses of symbolic environment seldom achieve.

I have dwelt on this kind of condensation because I think it helps to explain why James can manage his insistent centripetal motion without losing the solid world. It might be tempting, in theoretical abstraction from the actual novels, to suggest that Tolstoy's moths in the lawyer's room in *Anna Karenina* have a solidity which James's insistently symbolic objects lack. James manages, in fact, to combine the significance objects hold for the character with the sense of their objective significance. It is rather like the way we make personal symbols in real life, taking the weather or the object or the happy and unhappy coincidence in a way which confesses the arbitrariness of our act of fanciful interpretation. 'This is what it seems to imply' we say, without taking the symbolic reading too seriously. I do not suggest that James always makes his symbolic references in this way, and indeed his use of the Dove and the Golden Bowl is a very different and more conventionally 'conceited' mode of generalization which totally absorbs the object in the symbol. But the bulk of James's generalization is done in this way, by scenes rather than metaphors, or by scenes which provide a literal source for metaphor at the same time as preserving their immediacy and particularity. This is not a novel where the central obsession gives us a claustrophobic world within the mind. Anyone who knows Robbe-Grillet will see the difference.

Milly's consciousness is of course not always central, not always the narrative register. There is another striking use of appropriate environment much later in the novel, when in Chapter xxx it is Merton Densher who is tormented by solitude and uncertainty. He is turned away for the first time from the Palazzo Leporelli, and while Eugenio explains that the ladies are 'a "leetle" fatigued', it is, characteristically, what is not said as well as what is said which has a sinister quality:

They stood for a long minute facing each other over all they didn't say. . . . It was a Venice all of evil that had broken out for them alike, so that they were together in their anxiety, if they really could have met on it; a Venice of cold, lashing rain from a low black sky, of wicked wind raging through narrow passes, of general arrest and interruption, with the people engaged in all the water-life huddled, stranded and wageless, bored and cynical, under archways and bridges.

And, a page later:

Here, in the high arcade, half Venice was crowded close, while, on the Molo, at the limit of the expanse, the old columns of St. Mark and of the Lion were like the lintels of a door wide open to the storm. It was odd for him, as he moved, that it should have made such a differ-ence—if the difference wasn't only that the palace had for the first time failed of a welcome. There was more, but it came from that; that gave the harsh note and broke the spell. The wet and the cold were now to reckon with, and it was precisely, to Densher, as if he had seen the obliteration, at a stroke, of the margin of a faith in which they were all living. The margin had been his name for it—for the thing that, though it had held out, could bear no shock. The shock, in some form, had come, and he wondered about it while, threading his way among loungers as vague as himself, he dropped his eyes sightlessly on the rubbish in shops. There were stretches of the gallery paved with squares of red marble, greasy now with the salt spray; and the whole place, in its huge elegance, the grace of its conception and the beauty of its detail, was more than ever like a great drawing-room, the drawing-room of Europe, profaned and bewildered by some reverse of fortune. He brushed shoulders with brown men whose hats askew, and the loose sleeves of whose pendent jackets, made them resemble melancholy maskers.

This description of Venice smudged by rain, its inhabi-tants at a loss, is, like the scene in Regent's Park, carefully placed between two climaxes. Before it comes the denial at the Palazzo, and after it the glimpse of Lord Mark. The denial makes Densher know that something has happened, seeing Lord Mark tells him what has happened: 'The weather had changed, the rain was ugly, the wind wicked, the sea impossible, *because* of Lord Mark. It was because of him, *a fortiori* that the palace was closed.' He does not learn the details of Lord Mark's disclosures until he is told by Susan Shepherd Stringham who knows by intuition, but he knows enough. The wandering in the rain, with 'the broken charm of the world about . . . broken into smaller pieces' continues during the three days between seeing Lord Mark and being visited by Mrs Stringham. When she turns up she too is viewed as part of the appropriate appearance of things, for 'It appeared a part of her weight that she was in a wet waterproof . . . and that her face, under her veil, richly rosy with the driving wind, was—and the veil too—as splashed as if the rain were her tears.'

This is one of the most elaborate pieces of symbolic description in the novel, with a mobile, cinematic use of sympathetic weather and vague anonymous passers-by. Both feeling and technique might belong to a film by Antonioni. Once more the external world mirrors the sensations of the character, once more a shock within is shown in terms of a violent change without, once more the slow and gradual groping of inner reflection is worked out and defined by the aid of significant appearances. For the reader there is the shock of the change in Venice. The breaking of the charm is as violent as the deliberate change of Milly's surroundings from the rich protective world of drawing-room and chariot to the shabby exposure of the park. Once more it is the character who makes the interpretation. James puts the symbolic values in his own words rather more than he does in the earlier episode but I have quoted enough to show that the burden of the interpretation is Densher's. Once more the scene and the sensations are intimately fused, and in the fusion the symbolic transference does not obliterate the solid presences of the streets and weather and people. Densher is given the right place, the right neighbours, and the right conditions for formulating his shock and fear. He is also given something precise to do and somewhere precise to do it, so that his claustrophobic obsession, reminding us of Milly's, has a local habitation.

There is, finally, an excellent example of the two-faced Jamesian dialogue which is plausible on the surface but bristling with hidden meanings, in the recognition scene between Densher and Mrs Stringham. We first see Mrs Stringham's waterproof and her wet face, and at the end of their long dialogue, where tension is largely the product of what is read between the lines, there is a good small example of James's ability to make a symbol without loss of definiteness. Someone once said in a discussion of symbolic interpretation that we had got to the point where a character could not turn on the light without something being made of it, and at the end of Chapter xxxi, Densher asks if lights shall be lit:

> Dusk was now deeper, and after he had once more taken counsel of the dreariness without he turned to his companion. 'Shall we have lights—a lamp or the candles?'
> 'Not for me.'
> 'Nothing?'
> 'Not for me.'

Any comment on the delicacy of this seems clumsy. I will only say that if the Venetian scenes seem over-elaborate or in any way melodramatic, the weight of this brief passage is the product of great restraint. It is done by sheer infectious tension, by the unspoken words, by the context of the revelation, and the sense of shame and irrevocability. By now a mere detail like the 'the dreariness without' and the repetition of 'Not for me' tips us over from a mere sense of time and place and atmosphere, from an impression of a protective dimness for which Densher feels grateful, to the recognition of a larger darkness. It is a recognition which does not signal furtively to the reader behind the backs of the characters, but which is their recognition too.

'Try to be one of the people on whom nothing is lost', is James's advice to the novice in *The Art of Fiction* and his world of intense and total relevance is the imprint of characters on whom nothing is lost. In this way he achieves the concentration of appearances and larger meanings, the concentration of narration and action within character, and— something I have not mentioned but which is familiar to every reader of James—the concentration of past and future in the present tense. The sensibility of the characteristic Jamesian centre of consciousness is not merely a power of moral insight. The moral vision of decency is often very slowly and painfully purchased, as in the case of Densher, and is made dependent on something like the sensibility of the critic. There are few symbolic objects or scenes or persons in James which are not fairly explicitly interpreted by the characters themselves.

CHAPTER II

The Matter and the Treatment:
Henry James

'THERE is life and life', James says in his Preface to *The Tragic Muse*, 'and as waste is only life sacrificed and thereby prevented from "counting" I delight in a deep-breathing economy and an organic form.' James is supporting form as the appropriate means to the end of representing life, but when we come to look closely at both theory and practice this relationship of means and end turns out to be neither easy nor coherent. Perhaps we should look first at his romantic terminology. 'Organic form' is a term which has outlived its usefulness, at least if it is used without qualification and copious tests. There is a character in Malcolm Bradbury's *Eating People is Wrong*, who disconcerts his Professor by asking in a seminar, 'What is organic form?' and who goes on to argue, awkwardly and soundly, that if we cut off an arm, the man may live, but if we cut off his head, he will die. It is usually difficult to distinguish head from arm in James. His 'organic forms' lack the graduation of the natural organism for he is, as I have already suggested, luxuriating in difficulties which arise necessarily in the drama but which are a more gratuitous discipline in the novel. The kind of characteristic condensation I have been discussing is by no means essential to narrative, and most novelists have managed with a looser structure, dividing the modes and the effects in a way foreign to James. The play has to economize on time and effects, and cannot use its author's voice directly. The closest analogy to James's art comes from the cinema, and not the theatre, though in both film and theatre the visual medium has to be at once intensely realistic and symbolic.

James is also much more aware of creating a beautiful form than most novelists have been, and here again the analogy which is most useful comes from the unliterary arts, from painting or sculpture or music, where the delights are more sensuously immediate than in most novels, and where the formal appearances are not merely received as means to the end of expression but are apprehended as pleasureable. The balance-loving, antithetical nature of man finds more satisfaction in a novel by James than in one by Dickens or George Eliot, where the form is less visible and more functionally subordinate. Even where James is talking of the effects of a strict compression and unity he is very much concerned with the aesthetic delight which the pattern may produce as pattern and not as means.

He says, at the end of the Preface to *The Tragic Muse*, that though the novel did not entirely fulfil his intentions, since Nick Dormer 'insisted in the event on looking as simple and flat as some mere brass check or engraved number', it succeeds in its 'preserved and achieved unity . . . of tone':

That preserved and achieved unity and quality of tone, a value in itself, which I referred to at the beginning of these remarks. What I mean by this is that the interest created, and the expression of that interest, are things kept, as to kind, genuine and true to themselves. The appeal, the fidelity to the prime motive, is, with no little art, strained clear (even as silver is polished) in a degree answering—at least by intention—to the air of beauty. (*The Art of the Novel*, ed. R. P. Blackmur, p. 97)

The question of the beauty of narrative form is not one I wish to discuss here, but we must bear in mind, when praising and blaming James, that his ideas of formal economy are based on an unusually aesthetic and dramatic intention. It would surely be a besotted Jamesian who always insisted that this kind of economy had no disadvantages, and

James himself admitted that in particular instances there was a sacrifice of life to his requirements of form. It would be a besotted Jamesian who attempted to explain the passion for economy solely in terms of the dramatic and aesthetic purposes, who saw in every case of concentration the appropriate moral imprint we can find in the passages I have quoted from *The Wings of the Dove*. This passion may sometimes strike us as a spinsterly dislike of loose ends, especially when we see it, outside the accomplished novel, in the preliminaries of the notebooks. When we compare James's analysis of his art and materials with the less literary despairs of Tolstoy and D. H. Lawrence, his formal obsession seems appropriate to a writer living so entirely in and for his art. Like his predilection for the renounced relationship, it may arouse some suspicion.

Before moving on to the discussion of his failures—many of them self-acknowledged—I should like to look at one of the most powerful defences of formal economy. It betrays perhaps some unconscious suggestion of the limitations of this highly disciplined art. The defence is supplied by another novelist, a friend and contemporary of James working in very different areas of human experience but working to the same rigorous standards of form and style:

Mr. James utters his mind with a becoming fervour on the sanctity of truth to the novelist; on a more careful examination truth will seem a word of debatable propriety, not only for the labours of the novelist, but for those of the historian. No art—to use the daring phrase of Mr. James—can successfully 'compete with life'; and the art that does so is condemned to perish *montibus aviis*. Life goes before us, infinite in complications; attended by the most various and surprising meteors; appealing at once to the eye, to the ear, to the mind—the seat of wonder, to the touch—so thrillingly delicate, and to the belly—so imperious when starved. It combines and employs in its manifestation the method and the material, not of one art only, but of all the arts. Music is but an arbitrary trifling with a few of life's majestic chords; painting is but a shadow of its gorgeous pageantry of light and colour; literature does but drily indicate that wealth of incident, or moral obligation, of virtue, vice, action, rapture, and agony, with which it teems. . . .

What, then, is the object, what the method, of an art, and what the source of its power? The whole secret is that no art does 'compete with life'. Man's one method, whether he reasons or creates, is to half-shut his eyes against the dazzle and confusion of reality. The arts, like arithmetic and geometry, turn away their eyes from the gross, coloured, and mobile nature at our feet, and regard instead a certain figmentary abstraction. Geometry will tell us of a circle, a thing never found in nature; asked about a green circle or an iron circle, it lays its hand upon its mouth. . . . For the welter of impressions, all forcible but discrete, which life presents, it substitutes a certain artificial series of impressions, all indeed most feebly represented, but all aiming at the same effect, all eloquent of the same idea, all chiming together like consonant notes in music or like the graduated tints in a good picture. For all its chapters, from all its pages, from all its sentences, the well-written novel echoes and re-echoes its one creative and controlling thought; to this must every incident and character contribute; the style must be pitched in unison with this; and if there is anywhere a word that looks another way, the book would be stronger, clearer, and (I had almost said) fuller without it. Life is monstrous, infinite, illogical, abrupt, and poignant; a work of art, in comparison, is neat, finite, self-contained, rational, flowing, and emasculate.[1]

This is Robert Louis Stevenson's *Humble Remonstrance*, which was published in *Longman's Magazine* in December 1884, in reply to James's essay *The Art of Fiction* which had appeared there in September of the same year. James had been attacking Walter Besant's exaggerated claims for the artistry of fiction, and had pleaded for the importance of the novelist's sense of reality and 'solidity of specification'. 'The only classification of the novel that I can understand', he said, 'is into that which has life and that which has it not', and a little later we find him insisting that 'catching the strange irregular rhythm of life . . . is the attempt whose

---

[1] Reprinted in *Henry James and Robert Louis Stevenson*, ed. Janet Adam Smith, pp. 89–92.

strenuous force keeps Fiction upon her feet.' This essay, perhaps the most theoretical discussion of his art, must be read together with his Prefaces, written more than twenty years later.

In the Preface to *The Tragic Muse*, we find him admitting that *The Newcomes* and *Les Trois Mousquetaires* and *Peace and War* [*sic*] have 'life' and adding the stern question, 'but what do such large loose baggy monsters, with their queer elements of the accidental and the arbitrary, artistically *mean*?' Life is no longer enough. James's 'strange irregular rhythm of life' is not really inconsistent with Stevenson's rejection of the abrupt and the illogical, though his choice of phrase may have played its part in provoking Stevenson's clearer defence of their common pursuit. Stevenson's eloquent plea for concentration and total relevance defines the limitations of 'life' and if Prose Fiction had a Muse these are the accents in which she would speak to James and Turgenev and Stevenson himself. They are, however, not her only accents, and in order to recognize her catholicity we should put beside them not merely the practice of the large loose Victorians and the Russians but the spirited defence of truth and rejection of artistry made by D. H. Lawrence. As we shall see, it is Lawrence who passionately advocated a medium which should express just that illogicality and abruptness and monstrosity which Stevenson accepted in life but excluded from literature.

The novelist who tries to give us the green or the iron circle is indeed sacrificing the clear assertion of circularity, but the novelist who concentrates on a single feature makes sacrifices too. It is obvious from James's Prefaces that he was certainly not unaware of the many special dangers and difficulties of his search for economy. In his essay on *The Art of Fiction* he insists that form and content are inseparable, though in a context where he is attacking the notion that there is 'a part of the novel which is the story and part of it which for mystical reasons is not.' But when he is discussing the characters of his novels he finds it possible to make another distinction, and indeed resents the blindness of those naïve critics who do not see it:

> It is a familiar truth to the novelist, at the strenuous hour, that, as certain elements in any work are of the essence, so others are only of the form; that as this or that character, this or that disposition of the material, belongs to the subject directly, so to speak, so this or that other belongs to it but indirectly—belongs intimately to the treatment. This is a truth, however, of which he rarely gets the benefit—since it could be assured to him, really, but by criticism based upon perception, criticism which is too little of this world. (*The Art of the Novel*, pp. 53–4)

And he goes on to discuss the 'superabundance' of Henrietta Stackpole, in *The Portrait of a Lady*. In the Prefaces he is plainly aware of the difficulties involved in placing a character in the right formal position *and* preserving the necessary life. The failure of Mary Garland, in *Roderick Hudson*, he describes as a sacrifice of life to form:

> The difficulty had been from the first that I required my antithesis to Christina Light, one of the main terms of the subject. One is ridden by the law that antitheses, to be efficient, shall be both direct and complete. Directness seemed to fail unless Mary should be, so to speak 'plain', Christina being essentially so 'coloured'; and completeness seemed to fail unless she too should have her potency. (*The Art of the Novel*, p. 18)

We might perhaps question James's formulation of this 'law' that antitheses should be direct and complete. George Eliot and Tolstoy and D. H. Lawrence all confront his challenge with character-antithesis which make the categories clear while allowing for qualifications and incompleteness. But while this sense of 'law' is characteristic, so also is his test of life. He suggests that Mary's failure, which is the product of a complete antithesis, is a grave one, since we are just not convinced that Mary would be capable of casting such a spell on Roderick at a time when he is also under the spell of his sense of artistic power and opportunity, 'at a moment of the liveliest other preoccupation'. 'The damage to verisimilitude', says James, 'is deep.' He felt that he had failed again in handling the antithesis of place in the same novel, and finds in his treatment of Northampton, Mass. another unfortunately unbalanced weak term. There are many examples of the same stringent test of life, and of the same acknowledgement of the dangers of his own peculiar formalism in his criticism of *The American*. He tells us that he was 'so possessed' of his germinal idea of Newman's betrayal that he 'attached too scant an importance to its fashion of coming about' and admits that the portrait of Madame de Cintré and many individual scenes, show a cursoriness or an implausibility which wreck the novel. Once more his distinction between form and essence is crucial, and he sees his hero as the predetermined 'lighted figure' surrounded by a lamentable obscurity.

This distinction between characters belonging to the essence and characters belonging to the form is not necessarily one peculiar to all novels or even to all forms of concentrated narrative. We do not find it often in Hardy, with the possible exception of his rustic choruses, who might usefully be contrasted with George Eliot's and who are both essentially and formally functional. It might perhaps help us to describe some of the features of the novels of Defoe and Charlotte Brontë and E. M. Forster, all very different artists working in a very restricted form. In Defoe's novels we usually see one essential and vivid character in a world of functional shadows, and we might complain that Jane Eyre is 'of the essence' and Rochester, at least in his moral conversion, too crudely 'of the form'. The distinction, however, is one which I think breaks down in the face of the novels of George Eliot and Dickens and Tolstoy, where there is an initial or fundamental imaginative refusal to discriminate between characters who are major and those who are minor terms. The multiple action gives lavish opportunity to develop an essential character in one story and use him as a functional character in another, and the very appearance of Lydgate or Oblonsky as minor terms in the story of Dorothea or Anna gives a special and truthful irony to the shifting pattern. This is to express the difference between Mary Garland and Lydgate or Oblonsky in mechanical and quantitative terms, and though we may observe that the multiple plot lends itself to an economical double use of characters, so that they may be central and functional, major and minor, this is clearly not the whole story.

It seems more appropriate to speak of an undivided imaginative sense of character running through the whole hierarchy of the pattern, rather than of the opportunities of the multiple action. There are indeed minor characters who have no central position, no story of their own, but who are still so brilliantly and warmly particularized that there seems to be no distinction between form and essence. There are characters who have an important part to play as agents or messengers, plot-characters like Bartle Massey in *Adam Bede* or Klesmer in *Daniel Deronda*, who strike us as being created out of the same loving identification as main characters such as Adam and Gwendolen. There are characters described by James as fools, 'fools who minister, at a particular crisis, to the intensity of the free spirit engaged with them'. When Mrs Poyser ministers to Dinah's intensities, or Oblonsky to Karenin's, the minor characters not only appear as intense and alive, but actually function in this kind of contrast by virtue of their own experience and their capacity for response and feeling.

When James is discussing the character of Maria Gostrey, in *The Ambassadors*, to whom I shall return later, he speaks of the need to dissimulate bare function, to disguise the character belonging to the form and not to the essence. It does not seem appropriate to say that George Eliot and Tolstoy are simply very successful in this kind of dissimulation. Shakespeare's functional characters like Mercutio and

Enobarbus seem to be cases of dazzling disguise, but when we look at both their personality and their dramatic role Shakespeare appears to be performing an act of strict subordination, so that the vividness of the minor figure is there to animate the function. Neither character is shown at length in independent action: even the treacherous flight and death of Enobarbus is made with complete reference to Antony's central position and problem. Where James succeeds with his functional characters it is as the dramatist succeeds, with an appearance of vivid life but no suggestion of action outside the frame of the concentrated form. Jim Pocock is an excellent lively parody of Strether, presenting a vulgar knowingness about the advantages of Paris which throws both the narrowness of Woollett and the finer moral discriminations of Strether into high relief. He exists only within this function. The Assinghams in *The Golden Bowl* provide a varied chorus, fully delineated within the limits of the function, reacting with insight and blindness, possessiveness and responsibility, acting as agents, commentators, and prophets. There is absolutely nothing in their characters or relationship or social position which conveys any sense of larger existence. Their 'poverty', their detachment, and their childlessness are never described except as equipment for their function. A character like Catherine Arrowpoint in *Daniel Deronda*, or Varenka in *Anna Karenina*, fulfils a function of antithesis, plain to the reader and indeed explicitly noted by the 'major terms', Gwendolen and Kitty. But each is as substantial and sympathetic as the major characters, not just because they have many facets and vivid personalities, but also because they are shown with great economy, and the novelist has clearly little scope for showing them changing and developing on anything like the scale on which the major characters change and develop. But when Catherine is seen with Klesmer, the relationship asserts itself as moving and convincing in its own right, not as a mere mirror for the problems of the heroine. When

Varenka makes friends with Kitty, or is shown in her own abortive love-affair, the response which is brought about in the reader is a sympathy with the individual case. To describe Catherine Arrowpoint or Varenka, or even Mrs Poyser or Mr Brooke, entirely in terms of their contribution to plot and moral argument is to leave out a great deal of what they say and do, and to leave out also the impression of a world composed of individual lives, not of manipulated agents.

Henrietta Stackpole and Miss Barrace[1] have their loves and their careers, but these are treated very thinly and comically, belonging to a different mode from the medium of love which creates Isabel and Strether. They are also treated very sketchily, and tend to be invisible when not actually on the stage, whereas one of the details which testifies to the individual status of Catherine Arrowpoint, for instance, is the resonance which a mere mention of her name can bring. We know, in spite of brief treatment, that Catherine and Klesmer are going on with their satisfying and stable life, and there are vivid reminders of its continued existence. James at times even gives us the impression of cursory motivation, so that Miss Barrace's relationship with Waymarsh is nothing but a parody of Strether's with Maria Gostrey. His minor characters do not have a full weight of substantial life behind them and if this is economy and Varenka is 'waste', we should remember that economy can be mean and waste generous. I had better add that I agree with James and many other critics that George Eliot is certainly capable of failure. When she creates an inanimate character it is usually not because she has failed with a minor term but with a major term, and this too has its own significance.

One of James's doubtful minor terms is Maria Gostrey, and in the Preface to *The Ambassadors* he has several illuminating comments on her function and treatment:

[1] The fact that some of these functional characters had prototypes in life is interesting but irrelevant.

She is the reader's friend ... in consequence of dispositions that make him so eminently require one; and she acts in that capacity, and *really* in that capacity alone, with exemplary devotion, from beginning to end of the book. She is an enrolled, a direct, aid to lucidity; she is, in fine, to tear off her mask, the most unmitigated and abandoned of ficelles. Half the dramatist's art, as we well know—since if we don't it's not the fault of the proofs that lie scattered about us—is in the use of *ficelles*; by which I mean in a deep dissimulation of his dependence on them. (*The Art of the Novel*, p. 322)

He goes on, a little later, to say something about this dissimulation, and refers us to the last scene of the novel:

How and where and why to make Miss Gostrey's false connexion carry itself, under a due high polish, as a real one. Nowhere is it more of an artful expedient for mere consistency of form, to mention a case, than in the last 'scene' of the book, where its function is to give or to add nothing whatever, but only to express as vividly as possible certain things quite other than itself and that are of the already fixed and appointed measure. Since, however, art is all *expression*, and is thereby vividness, one was to find the door open to any amount of delightful dissimulation. ... To project imaginatively, for my hero, a relation that has nothing to do with the matter (the matter of my subject) but has everything to do with the manner (the manner of my presentation of the same) and yet to treat it, at close quarters and for fully economic expression's possible sake, as if it were important and essential—to do that sort of thing and yet muddle nothing may easily become, as one goes, a signally attaching proposition.... (op. cit. p.324)

Although James is fully aware that a functional character may be given inadequate life, and although he is fully aware that a functional character may engage too much of our interest (he thinks this happens in the case of Henrietta Stackpole) he does not, as far as I know, consider the possibility that a functional character may be given too much life, may step with impropriety outside the function, may be too heavily disguised. This problem may be implied in the 'yet muddle nothing' of the paragraph I have just quoted, but certainly James does not give an instance of this kind of muddle.

At the end of *The Ambassadors* James exploits his own marvellous devices of telepathic communication and the circumlocutory hint, to make Maria Gostrey propose to Strether and, with a little less evasion, to make Strether say no:

He had sufficiently understood. 'So good as this place at this moment? So good as what *you* make of everything you touch?' He took a minute to say, for, really and truly, what stood about him there in her offer—which was as the offer of exquisite service, of lightened care, for the rest of his days—might well have tempted. It built him softly round, it roofed him warmly over, it rested, all so firm, on selection. And what ruled selection was beauty and knowledge. It was awkward, it was almost stupid, not to seem to prize such things; yet, none the less, so far as they made his opportunity they made it only for a moment. She would moreover understand—she always understood.

That indeed might be, but meanwhile she was going on. 'There's nothing, you know, I wouldn't do for you.'

'Oh yes—I know.'

'There's nothing,' she repeated, 'in all the world.'

'I know. I know. But all the same I must go.' He had got it at last. 'To be right.'

'To be right?'

She had echoed it in vague deprecation, but he felt it already clear for her. 'That, you see, is my only logic. Not, out of the whole affair, to have got anything for myself.'

She thought. 'But with your wonderful impressions you'll have got a great deal.'

'A great deal'—he agreed. 'But nothing like *you*. It's you who would make me wrong!'

Honest and fine, she couldn't greatly pretend she didn't see it. Still, she could pretend just a little. 'But why should you be so dreadfully right?'

'That's the way that—if I must go—you yourself would be the first to want me. And I can't do anything else.'

So then she had to take it, though still with her defeated protest. 'It isn't so much your *being* "right"—it's your horrible sharp eye for what makes you so.'

'Oh but you're just as bad yourself. You can't resist me when I point that out.'

She sighed it at last all comically, all tragically, away. 'I can't indeed resist you.'

'Then there we are!' said Strether.

This scene of renunciation has more than the single function indicated by James. As well as dissimulating the functional thinness of Maria Gostrey it gives the last consistent turn of the screw in its demonstration of Strether's disinterestedness. He has learnt first the limitations of Woollett and then the limitations of the aesthetic sense of Paris. He has revised both his first prejudices about the effects of Europe on Chad, and then his hasty romantic view of Chad's superior refinements. Having cast off two illusions he is left to make the renunciation of any personal advantage—except the advantage of knowledge—which the affair has brought to him. But this last renunciation is made to appear strongly active, unlike his earlier reactions which have followed inevitably and more passively on seeing the facts. It is as if James were making the moral collocation he had earlier made in *The Portrait of a Lady*, where Isabel makes a similar advance in moral perception and ends with the last fine development showing itself in a painful open-eyed disregard of self. There is at least one vital difference between Isabel and Strether: she is involved in action in a way which he is not. He has his ambassadorial function, but in spite of the advice he gives to Little Bilham, and eventually to Chad, he has not been intimately involved in the relations he has observed and come to understand and appraise. The final renunciation has something gratuitous about it: having learnt that there is coarseness in Woollett and betrayal in Paris, he cannot himself learn to accept the future Maria proffers. James says in the Preface that this last scene gives and adds nothing, that the relation projected here has nothing to do with the matter and everything with the manner. This is a somewhat confusing gloss. The 'relation' implies a possible course of action, a practical choice, of the kind Strether has not had before. This may be to discriminate crudely between knowing and doing, in a way foreign to James, but even if we withdraw this discrimination, and rephrase the difference, there still seems to be some difficulty in accepting the possibilities of marriage for Strether, the observer who receives his education too late, and his admirable confidante. There is certainly moral consistency here. Strether is enacting the kind of disinterestedness which endorses his moral vision. He originally sees Chad as acting in the very way he himself failed to act as a young man, and his admiration and vicarious approval are loudly voiced in the famous scene where he advises Little Bilham to live. But by the time his education has been completed we have come to see the crudity of this advice. Chad's betrayal of Madame de Vionnet, which Strether knows is all but an accomplished fact, and his new-found vocation in advertising, have made it clear that Chad is not the kind of man who fairly represents a possible past might-have-been for Strether.

It is not just a question of James's failure in dissimulating Maria Gostrey's functional identity—that merely brings out the 'muddle' more clearly. Strether's education is, I suggest, made implausible in the interests of consistency and completeness, and verisimilitude has been sacrificed to the ruling idea. The conclusion, down to the last detail, is a symmetrical and final statement which takes us back to the beginning of the novel, but it is, unlike the end of *The Portrait of a Lady* and *The Wings of the Dove*, more symmetrical than likely. When have we been able to think of this kind of future for Strether? What view of his relation with Maria has presented itself which makes us able to see this last beautiful denial as a real renunciation at all?

James apparently considered the end successful, and if he had met the suggestion that it creates more difficulties than it smoothes away, he would presumably have accounted for the muddle by referring to Maria's disguise. But there is, I suggest, another reason, harking back to what I have been saying about the critical skills of his main characters. If it is Milly who most successfully interprets the symbolism which defines her, so it is Strether who—less successfully—interprets the moral structure of this book. If the novel had ended before the last scene, the critic might well have commented that this kind of middle-aged *Bildungsroman* movingly and appropriately uses the point of view of a disengaged spectator, whose sensibility rather than his actions convinces the reader that there is a kind of decency which Chad lacks and a kind of refinement which Mrs Newsome lacks. This last scene makes Strether put this perception into so many words, and the words are given the occasion of action. This falsification of action seems to me to impose an unnecessary strain on a great novel.

A similar unsuccessful gloss on the novel's implications is made at the end of *The Golden Bowl*. In this novel Charlotte is the only character who is excluded from revealing her centre of consciousness, and for that there may be certain internal reasons. Amerigo's intelligence and his moral superiority to Charlotte qualify him for playing his initial part as a sensitive though inadequate register of action. His narrative function reveals his goodwill, his innocence, his subtlety, and his capacity for a certain degree of insight. Adam Verver's much briefer appearance as narrative register is also both appropriate and necessary. Without his solitary vision we should see very much less clearly his need for Charlotte, his protective love for Maggie and, eventually, the ironical probability that while Maggie deceives and protects him he is doing the same for her. Maggie qualifies for the role of narrator at precisely that moment when she begins to see that something is happening, and her gradual discovery and decisions to remain silent and to lie take us along the characteristic track of doubt, glimmerings, and insight. Perhaps James does not use Charlotte because she would either tell us too much and rush us rapidly past the fine discriminations between her deceit and Amerigo's blunderings,[1] or, later, would tell us too little, since she is excluded from knowledge. She is, as Amerigo says, in one of those correlations of intelligence and moral integrity which may well make us feel uneasy, too stupid to record the subtlety of this moral action.

The form of the novel is most sensitively adapted to the relationships and developments of the characters, and Charlotte's exclusion, though it perhaps brings her a sympathy which blurs the final effect, is at least understandable. But the sympathy which so many readers have felt for Charlotte has, I think, more to do with the way James delegates his authorial summary to Maggie. When I spoke of the character acting as critic, I might equally well have spoken of the character acting as author. In the case of Milly Theale, the dramatic appropriateness of her critical insight seems perfect. In the case of Maggie something happens which is less successful. James does not choose to speak in his own voice, not at least when it comes to making explicit moral judgements, though he does not choose to leave these judgements to the reader. And it is Maggie who is given words which express Charlotte's function in the novel: 'She has been necessary to build us up', which is a remark which either author or critic might have made with better taste. On the lips of the woman who is defending her unsuccessful rival to the husband she has just won it seems a staggeringly selfish and complacent comment. I do not suggest that this one single comment strains the book: I think it is indeed a consistent and conveniently blatant example of the whole conception of Maggie. The conception seems to be flawed by James's refusal to let her be either simply biassed and jealous, as Jane Austen allows Fanny to be, in *Mansfield*

---

[1] For an account of these discriminations, see 'The Given Appearance of Charlotte Verver', by Elizabeth Owen, *Essays in Criticism*, Vol. XIII, No. 4, October 1963.

Park, after she has triumphed in not wholly dissimilar circumstances, or less intelligently articulate. No woman in Maggie's position would be in a state to make this kind of godlike comment with godlike disinterestedness. The tenderness and passion of the last triumphant embrace completes the pattern only at the expense of that sympathy which should allow us to rejoice at the Prince's words, 'I see only you'.

These are not the only places where James's characteristic concentration and economy is dearly purchased, but they are important and conveniently similar examples. Let me now add briefly, in tentative suggestions rather than full discussion, that other examples of implausibility are to be found in James's earlier dramatic novels like *The Spoils of Poynton*, *What Maisie Knew*, and *The Awkward Age*, all novels owing much to his experiments in drama, and all deliberate exercises in a restricted point of view and dialogue. In each case there is not merely strict economy but perfect and conspicuous symmetry: *The Awkward Age* was planned as a number of illuminating mirrors placed evenly round their centre, *What Maisie Knew* has the formality of a quadrille, in balance and in permutation, and *The Spoils of Poynton* has the basic irony of the fatal Spoils, worked out in an equipoise of irony and cross-purposes. Each novel purchases form at the expense of humanity: *The Awkward Age*, a novel first conceived as a short story and developing theme at top-heavy length, has the most embarrassing solution propounded in fiction. Its heroine is the sacrifice to English compromise, and her awkwardness such an impediment in love that she eventually turns to Mr Longdon for protection. Neither Van's sense of her awkwardness nor our response to the solution is more than cursorily handled. *What Maisie Knew* reduces appropriate feeling for the likely results of marital disaster to a brilliant exercise in plotting. The response of the child is exploited rather than properly delineated and the agility of form is achieved at the expense of feeling. *The Spoils of Poynton* is one of those stories where the original 'germ' was tiny in relation to the final product, and in the Preface we can trace James's slow development of the fitting human action, first hitting on Fleda's consciousness, then on her relations with Owen. The original bright idea was the irony of the all-powerful Spoils, their value, their theft, and their badly timed return, and the human action is developed as manner rather than matter, to use James's distinction. Not all the characters are sufficiently subdued to the ironical fatality of the Spoils, and Fleda's renunciation of Owen, her change of mind, and his capitulation (off stage) to the terrible Mona Brigstock have a thinness of motivation, explicable possibly by their subordinated mechanical position. The important thing— to judge from the reports of James's planning and from the results—is not the human action but the planned and external destiny. The over-valued Spoils and Mrs Gereth's clever but 'not intelligent' bargaining with them have substance and conviction, and the relationships of Fleda, Owen, and Mona are not exactly implausible—the renunciations, changes, and capitulation are all possible events—but are cursorily worked out in the particular terms of the novel, appearing too conveniently present as occasions for the main irony rather than convincing in their own right. Mrs Gereth has to believe strongly enough in the possibilities of Owen's love for Fleda in order to send the Spoils back to Poynton. The final outcome is predetermined by the original idea, and must be one of ironical loss. Fleda's first renunciation, her change of mind, and Mona's victory, are as subordinated to the planned plot as Jude's death is subordinated to the ideological pattern. In *The Spoils of Poynton* there is a cursoriness of motivation which makes the relation of end and means starkly apparent. We may want to say the same about the suicide and the murders of Father Time, but it would be difficult to say that the details of Jude's susceptibilities and Sue's frigidity are as flimsily specified.

At his best, in *The Portrait of a Lady* or *The Wings of the Dove*, James achieves his elegance and economy, as Hardy usually achieves his dogmatic illustration, without the loss of plausibility and particularity.

James's aesthetic obsession often betrays itself—and life—in his conclusions, where the expense of truth shows itself in the final symmetry or completion. But if the mannered aesthetic conclusions of *The Spoils of Poynton* and *The Ambassadors* are clear instances of aesthetic betrayal, excluding the illogical and the untidy at some cost, some of his novels are remarkable just for their triumphantly open and 'incomplete' endings, which at least appear to accommodate the abrupt and the unfinished rhythm of actual existence. James says himself, 'really, universally, relations stop nowhere, and the exquisite problem of the artist is eternally but to draw, by a geometry of his own, the circle within which they shall happily appear to do so' (*The Art of the Novel*). The metaphor of the geometrician and his circle, which was used by Stevenson, has different implications in different novels. James's narrative form is not conspicuous for its closure.

James seldom completes the circle by death or marriage, and those novels where these conventional endings appear have an air of finality of their own. This is true of *Roderick Hudson* (though Christina Light continued to solicit her author, with some success, for a future in another novel), in *Daisy Miller*, *The Princess Casamassima* and *The Bostonians*. In many of the other novels the conclusion is less that of a climax in action, like a death or a marriage, than a dissolution of local tension. This is usually both a moral solution and the end to a certain set of social relations. The charmed circle is broken in *The Awkward Age*, and although Nanda's future is uncertain we know what it will *not* be like. The same thing applies to the last three novels, where a particular set of relationships, which have constituted the action and the structure, come to an end. The intricate dance is over, and the survivors left, either in isolation, as in *The Wings of the Dove*, or in a very different relation, as in *The Golden Bowl*. Most commonly, we have the isolated individual, who has learnt a lesson which involves a clean break.

The 'open' endings of *The Portrait of a Lady* and *The Wings of the Dove* leave us in some uncertainty. We do not know what will happen to Isabel Archer, merely that she will return to her husband, having been exposed to the fullest temptation of passionate love.[1] We do not know what will happen to Kate and Merton Densher, merely that their relationship has been made impossible by the one event they longed for and worked for. But all that we do not know is the detail of the future, and in Isabel's case we have some grim suggestions remaining from the action that has been set before us. The important thing is not left doubtful—the moral issue is absolutely clear. Strether can have nothing for himself, having seen the cruel consequences of selfishness. Kate and Densher can never again be as they were. Isabel sees a straight path. James not only shows this but makes it morally explicit. The line he draws at the end of these novels is not at all like the line cut by the frame of an impressionist painting, suggesting the arbitrary limits of the impression. Nor is it like the head emerging from the rough unworked block, implying the struggle with the raw material. Nor again is it like the line drawn at the end of *Anna Karenina* or *Women in Love* or *Lady Chatterley's Lover* which draws our attention to inconclusiveness and the onward flow. This appearance of an invitation to speculate further has its own completeness: if we make the attempt we are brought up against the lack of cues and against the moral finality. James does not give us the detailed guarantee for the future which we find at the end of *Hard Times*—one of Dickens's best endings—or at the end of *Middlemarch*. Such guarantees rest on the convention that everything of moral importance has happened to these people. They may go on having

---

[1] This is how I read Isabel's last encounter with Caspar Goodwood.

children and working but there will be no more crises. James is setting his concentrated story in a more realistic context than this. It belongs to the world where there is no end to change and crisis. But the moral guarantee he does give us, explicitly and completely. The end is no question-mark, no trailing forward, but an underlining which takes us back more intensely to the story we have witnessed. It is the last turn of the screw which gives the tightest ending to his concentrated form.

CHAPTER III

Dogmatic Form:
Defoe, Charlotte Brontë,
Thomas Hardy, and E. M. Forster

HENRY JAMES's distinction between matter and treatment provides a useful answer to critics who like to regard the form of a novel as equivalent to its total expression. Both in theory and practice James distinguishes characters and details which are functional and subordinate from characters and details which are of primary importance. He also makes it necessary for us to consider narrative form as aesthetically conspicuous and satisfying. These distinctions, I have suggested, sometimes result in a failure to reconcile the urge for composition with the urge for truthfulness. But there are other conflicts in the art of fiction, and other instances of restricted truthfulness. In this chapter I want to consider a group of novels whose range is restricted by a common pressure. This is the pressure of dogmatism, at first sight entirely different from the pressures at work in the novels of James.

I want to exploit both the neutral descriptive sense of the word dogmatism and its pejorative connotations. Defoe, Charlotte Brontë, Hardy, and E. M. Forster are all novelists who use their art to embody an ideology. Because of the very nature of the ideology, their art shapes character and action in a special way.

If we use the word dogmatic in its neutral sense we should probably say that most interesting novels have a dogmatic form, organizing their action and characters with a systematic moral significance. When Dickens classifies individuals and families and institutions according to their capacity for love and true charity, as he does in *Bleak House*, the novel has a dogmatic form. When George Eliot presents her characters in the recognizable categories of selfishness and unselfishness, as she does in all her novels, her form is dogmatic. The form of such ethical classification does not necessarily make the detail of character and action unrealistic, though we might argue that some distortion of truth is usually involved. The optimism of Dickens and the meliorism of George Eliot, as argued and demonstrated in their novels, rely heavily on the moral fallacy of consistent progress and deterioration. But this fallacy only becomes conspicuous when we look at the implications of their work as a whole, and measure it against the complexities of our experience. The progress and deterioration is usually convincing within single novels. Even George Eliot, who is always appealing to general experience, proffers a selected group of cases, a story of certain individuals, not a mass survey covering the whole variety of human life. Both George Eliot and Dickens present us with individual cases, however typical these cases may appear to be, and we cannot easily accuse them of single-minded or simple-minded distortion. We may say that the consistent conversions on which their actions turn make human nature appear to be remarkably and systematically malleable, but we cannot say that all events and characters are propelled in one direction. There are relatively few shifts and reflexes in the moral pattern, but there are cases of deterioration as well as cases of improvement. There is intransigent material as well as malleable material. Human nature moves in many directions, and responds to the various influences of chance, heredity, environment, and individual relationships. Although we may finally object that the human race is presented as much more comprehensible and manageable than it actually is, there remains in novels like these some freedom and much variety.

In the case of the dogmatic forms which concern me here, there is a single and simplified belief which excludes much of the varied causality to be found in life, which is metaphysical in character and has precise moral consequences. In *Robinson Crusoe* and *Jane Eyre* the action and characters are shaped by the dogmatism of a special belief, the belief in Providence. In *Jude the Obscure* the action and characters are organized as illustrations of the opposite belief, in an absence of Providence which allows nature and society to frustrate the individual and create a pattern not significantly different from one which would illustrate a malignant God. E. M. Forster uses his characters and actions to illustrate more tentatively the possible sources of faith in meaningful existence. Just as James may on occasion make his selection from life restricted or implausible in order to make the novel dramatically shapely and concentrated, so these four novelists make their selected life conform, in similar restriction or implausibility, to their belief in the presence or absence of a powerful and practical Providence. Yet James usually succeeds in making his symmetry and economy express life without falsification, and Defoe and Charlotte Brontë and Hardy succeed, to a large extent, in reconciling dogma and realism. They write novels, not tracts. Their characters and actions are more than merely illustrative.

The presence of more than merely illustrative form is in part explained by the existence of more than one formative principle in the novel. When I speak of dogmatic form, I do not mean to suggest that these novels are exclusively dogmatic, like *Animal Farm*, and *1984*, where there is no tension between form and life, and no more than a single principle of dogmatic illustration. My examples are chosen either because they seem to me to represent such a tension, or because they have enough truthfulness to make them viable as particularized imitations of life, as novels.

In Ian Watt's excellent account of *Robinson Crusoe*, we find the suggestion that Defoe's Protestantism is in all important respects compatible with individualism and secular values. Watt says: 'If, for instance, we turn to the actual effect of Crusoe's religion on his behaviour, we find that it has curiously little' (*The Rise of the Novel*, p. 80). He suggests that Crusoe is not finally punished for his original filial disobedience, but indeed does rather well out of it, and goes on to comment that the frequent Providential interpretations of events are similarly divorced from the action. I would of course agree with Watt that much of the interest of the novel lies in the economic implications and the solid verisimilitude, but I would place a rather different interpretation on the importance of Providence. It is true that Crusoe does very well out of his filial disobedience, but only in the long run, and it seems odd to say that 'no real retribution follows', though it is consistent with Watt's later comment that Defoe disregarded 'the actual psychological effects of solitude'. It is perfectly true that Crusoe stands up to his long period of solitary confinement with extraordinary stamina, but I do not think it is true to say that the isolation, perils, and physical hardships of what Defoe explicitly calls 'the Island of Despair' are disregarded. Once we recognize the horrors of the island, the Providential pattern appears to be rather more closely integrated with the action and character, for the island is presented as Crusoe's ordeal, a punishment for filial disobedience and a purgatorial peril which he confronts with triumph. He does well in the long run not in spite of his original disobedience but because he has come through the ordeal and punishment, which, like many punishments in literature, is therapeutic and ultimately beneficial. *Robinson Crusoe* is composed of many pressures, but the main rhythm which shapes the adventures and solid details is the rhythm of a conversion. Its detail is not psychological, but it is a development novel. It follows the progress of the hero, the prodigal son who defies sound paternal advice and augury, who suffers, repents, and is rewarded. There is nothing very strange about this progress, and it is in main outline very close to its Biblical analogue. It might be possible to complain that the Prodigal Son did very well out of his disobedience too, but this is rather the partial view of his brother than the final moral implication of the parable.

The progress of the hero is divided into three stages: the initial defiance, the subsequent ordeal, and the final reward. These stages overlap, for the ordeal is not remitted as soon as Robinson Crusoe repents and prays in repentance and faith, but becomes a long and strenuous education in repentance and faith. It is, I suggest, the relation between the hero and his Providence which gives form to what would otherwise be a mere episodic record of adventure and endurance. Providence is the source of the early perils and warnings and the storm, shipwreck, fever, despair, and solitary confinement. When Robinson Crusoe turns in his despair and delirium and fear (as Martin Chuzzlewit was later to turn in his despair and delirium) to prayer and repentance and faith, Providence then begins to provide, though still in conditions which are often fearful and painful. Religious maxims are dramatized in the literal provisions of Providence, which helps him who helps himself, spreading a table in the wilderness. The wilderness is still a wilderness, and if Crusoe's mind endures with remarkable and implausible strength, Defoe gives enough space to his sufferings in solitude. 'Where Providence is bringing blessings', Watt observes, 'Crusoe need only accept' (ibid., p. 81), but Crusoe himself insists that he has to earn and use his blessings. There may at times be suggestions of idyllic solitude which makes it possible for Watt to describe the island as a 'Utopia' illustrating the need and holiness of solitude, but there are also many suggestions of its disadvantages. Fear remains and Crusoe's relationship with his God, as he repeatedly insists, does not make up for the absence of human beings, but as far as the reader is concerned, his relationship with Providence acts as a kind of surrogate, structurally and dramatically, for the human interplay which is the stuff of most fiction.

Until Robinson Crusoe saves Friday, his actions are all considered in relation to Providence. Providence communicates with him and influences events in ways which give variety to the action as well as continually illustrating the beneficence of God. This close relationship between God and the hero begins after the earthquake and fever and the warning vision of the man descending from the black cloud, spear in hand and threatening death. Crusoe's 'stupidity of soul' is pierced and he penitently reviews his past life, remembering his father's prediction, '*That if I did take this foolish step, God would not bless me, and I would have leisure hereafter to reflect upon having neglected his Counsel*'. He makes his first genuine prayer, '*Lord be my Help, for I am in great distress*'.

From that moment onwards, beginning with his acceptance of Providence and his question-and-answer with conscience on June 28, all the actions are interpreted as Providentially directed. He finds a roll of tobacco, and a Bible, a cure 'both for Soul and Body', and concludes that he has been 'directed by Heaven no doubt'. He ceases to pray for delivery from the island and finds out its fruitfulness. It is religious conversion which explains Robinson Crusoe's highly implausible endurance of solitary confinement, and which underlies his enterprise and prosperity. It is not until he achieves faith that he comes to regularize his life, for as he has 'observ'd no Sabbath-Day' he has 'omitted to distinguish the Weeks . . . and so did not really know what any of the Days were'. He applies the new-found sense of time and regularity to the seasons, and learns to divide them so as to provide accordingly. He substitutes daily reading and prayer for hysterical complaint, cannot quite bring himself to thank God for bringing him 'to this place' but manages to thank Him for opening his eyes to sin and bring about repentance 'by whatever afflicting providences'. He constantly interprets the island and his solitude in religious terms: he is removed from the world of lust, prodigality, mercenariness and ingratitude, and the isolation marks his formal rejection of worldly desires and expectations. In his reckoning of advantages Robinson Crusoe is a prototype Pollyanna, comparing what is bad with what might have been much worse: how much worse, for instance, would have been his fate 'if the good Providence of God had not wonderfully order'd the Ship to be cast up nearer the Shore', if he had been given his deserts instead of less punishment than he merited, if he had been cast away on some more savage shore, with 'furious Wolves or Tygers' or 'Savages to murther and devour'. As he comes to accept his providences and learns to hope for mercy, he recommends his trials and adventures as useful parables. Crusoe's faith, like the acute sensibility of a Jamesian character, allows him to make symbolic interpretation for the reader. This too is a concentrated form.

While he is casting up his reckoning he discovers that 'there was a strange Concurrence of Days, in the various Providences which befel me'. He ran away and was captured into slavery on the same day, escaped out of the Yarmouth Roads and from Sallee on the same day, and was cast up on the island on his birthday, 'so that my wicked Life, and my solitary Life begun both on a Day'. Crusoe anticipates the critic who wants to point out the archetypal rebirth pattern in the novel.

This symbolic interpretation prepares us for the appearance of the portents which are structurally important in the action. Prayer is answered by scripture or dream. When he has seen the footprint on the shore and Fear has banished religious Hope, he eventually composes himself to accept the event as a trial, decides to 'attend the Dictates and Directions of his daily Providence'. He finds that reassuring words of scripture come into his mind and that when he opens the Bible a hopeful text confronts him. The relationship of prayer and faith does not become easy or automatic, and soon there is a lapse into fear and his prayers come rather from terror than from 'Thankfulness, Love and Affection'. There is some oscillation: when he finds the horrid remains of the cannibal feast, he makes the best of it, just like Pollyanna, thanking God 'that had cast my first Lot in a Part of the World where I was distinguish'd from such dreadful Creatures as these'. He begins to be cautious about firing his gun, in case it should be heard, and marks the Providence which led him to furnish himself with his tame breed of goats. He notes also that the fear has checked his excessive interest in contrivance, 'taken off the Edge of my Invention for my own Conveniences' and led him to drop the 'whimsical' project of brewing. He is next led into military projects, inventing powder-traps and ambushes, but comes to accept the existence of the savages as Providentially ordained, gives up his inventions and thanks God for delivering him from 'Blood-Guiltiness', not without impassioned reflections on Spanish barbarities in America. The enterprise of the individual is checked and controlled.

The largest part of the novel is taken up with Robinson Crusoe's reflections and arguments, and his decisions, like his practical actions, are usually referred to Providence. I am not claiming that this is a subtle psychological novel, but I think it is misleading to praise it mainly for its external verisimilitude and economic significance. Robinson Crusoe's dialogue is not so much with himself as with another world, and just as the large pattern of his conversion is Providential, so the reflux of his thinking and feeling and deciding is expressed as his converse with spirits:

How when we are in (a *Quandary*, as we call it) a Doubt or Hesitation, whether to go this Way, or that Way, a secret Hint shall direct us this Way, when we intended to go that Way; nay, when

Sense, our own Inclination, and perhaps Business has call'd to go the other Way, yet a strange Impression upon the Mind, from we know not what Springs, and by we know not what Power, shall over-rule us to go this Way; and it shall afterwards appear, that had we gone that Way which we should have gone, and even to our Imagination ought to have gone, we should have been ruin'd and lost: Upon these, and many like Reflections, I afterwards made it a certain Rule with me, That whenever I found those secret Hints, or pressings of my Mind, to doing, or not doing any Thing that presented; or to going this Way, or that Way, I never fail'd to obey the secret Dictate. . . . (vol. i, p. 203)[1]

Robinson Crusoe's submission to the irrational voice is often dramatized by dreams and supernatural voices. Before his rescue of Friday, for instance, a great agitation and fear is followed by 'a sound Sleep' in which he dreams not of the fear, 'nor of any Thing relating to it', but of the escape of a victim of the cannibals who becomes his servant and pilot. The dream is followed by the practical decision to effect a rescue, and soon after in narrative time (though more than a year after in actual time) the dream and the decision meet in the rescue of Friday. Later, when the cannibals return, he first plans to attack them, then changes his mind, from religious scruple, and decides to do nothing 'unless something offer'd that was more a Call to me than yet I knew of'. This 'Call' comes when he sees that their victim is a white man, a European. The 'Call' leads to the rescue of the Spaniard and Friday's father.

The next crisis and warning comes when he sights the English longboat and his joy at seeing it is overcome by secret doubts:

Let no Man despise the secret Hints and Notices of Danger, which sometimes are given him, when he may think there is no Possibility of its being real. That such Hints and Notices are given us, I believe few that have made any Observations of things, can deny; that they are certain Discoveries of an invisible World, and a Converse of

---

[1] I have given page references to The Shakespeare Head Edition of *Robinson Crusoe* because of the absence of chapter divisions in the novel.

Spirits, we cannot doubt; and if the Tendency of them seems to be to
warn us of Danger, why should we not suppose they are from some
friendly Agent, whether supreme, or inferior, and subordinate, is not
the Question; and that they are given for our Good? (vol. ii, p. 41)

This secret admonition saves him once more. He rescues
the Captain and his two men, captures the mutinous crew,
and eventually sails to England, to find that his profits have
accumulated and that 'Providence has put into his hands' a
large estate. When he is later planning to go back to England
from Portugal he has another Providential warning:

I had been accustomed enough to the Sea, and yet I had a strange
Aversion to going to *England* by Sea at that time; and though I could
give no Reason for it, yet the Difficulty increas'd upon me so much,
that though I had once shipp'd my Baggage, in order to go, yet I
alter'd my Mind , and that not once, but two or three times.

It is true, I had been very unfortunate by Sea, and this might be
some of the Reason: But let no Man slight the strong impulses of his
own Thoughts in Cases of such Moment: Two of the Ships which I
had singl'd out to go in, I mean, more particularly singl'd out than
any other, that is to say, so as in one of them to have put my things on
Board, and in the other to have agreed with the Captain; I say, two of
these Ships miscarry'd, *viz.* One was taken by the *Algerines*, and the
other was cast away on the *Start* near *Torbay*, and all the People
drown'd except three; so that in either of these Vessels I had been
made most miserable; and in which most, it was hard to say. (vol. ii,
pp. 85–6)

The same Providential directions impel *The Farther
Adventures of Robinson Crusoe*, where it is clairvoyant dreams
sent by the converse of spirits which eventually send Crusoe
back to his island. Providence is in both parts of the story
more than a moral excursus, subordinate to adventure and
realistic detail. It is a strong governing principle of action
and psychology. Some of its moral implications are very
dubious. The hero's special Providence is often egocentric-
ally interpreted and there are notorious weak spots in the
morality, such as his lack of guilt about Xury and his excessive guilt about neglect of faith and prayer, the economic

and materialist implications, occasionally at odds with religion, but eventually reconciled, and the cheerful disregard of the victims who lie outside his special dispensation. The morality, though familiar enough in Nonconformist dogma and attitude outside Defoe, scarcely stands scrutiny, but it provides the novel not only with its main theme but with its principle of unity. The economic action, the adventures, and the long passages of reflection are linked and motivated by the Providential pattern. It is the dogma which is the source of the relationships between the beginning and middle and end, governing the temporal movement of the narrative, and it is the dogma which defines the morality and the hero's motives and actions. The narrative form is created by the ideology, and is happily compatible with the solid verisimilitude of external acts and facts. There is no tension between ideology and truth but the story has sufficient substance to convince and interest the reader.

There must be many novels where Providence is invoked to mark the successful resolution of difficulties, as in the conclusion of Smollett's *Roderick Random* and *Peregrine Pickle*, for instance, but Defoe, both in *Robinson Crusoe* and other novels, uses Providence not as a convenient *deus ex machina* in a story of little religious interest, but as an informing principle. When we come to the nineteenth century the concept of Providence is plainly outworn and discredited, and we find Dickens, George Eliot, and Meredith defining the egocentric or mercenary character by evoking just that faith in a *special* Providence which is taken for granted in Defoe. Podsnap, Casaubon, and Harry Richmond are examples of faith in discredited Providence, and this devaluation has an interesting place in novels which explore the responsibility and conflict of individuals and social relations. But in one of the most interesting early Victorian novels, *Jane Eyre*, Providence is still very much alive. The dubious moral implication of egocentricity and material profit are gone but the formal implications remain much the same. Providence is not a dead word when used by Charlotte Brontë, and it is no accident that she wrote that Providence had decreed her marriage with Arthur Nicolls and wrote a novel which is structurally very like *Robinson Crusoe*. There is the same rising intonation of optimistic faith, the same pattern of prayer and answer, and a very similar intercession of dreams, portents, and coincidences. *Jane Eyre*, however, is not a novel about religious conversion, and perhaps this is to be regretted.

Jane is like Crusoe in her disregard of Heaven. What he puts first is adventure, what she puts first is human love. Her early passionate sense of injustice is rebuked by Helen Burns, who refers her to the approval of conscience and the kingdom of spirits and warns her, 'You think too much of the love of human beings'. Although Jane's conversion to Helen's values is cursorily treated, and indeed taken for granted in her discovery of value and activity as pupil and teacher at Lowood, by the time she comes to leave we have reached the second stage of the action, where prayer is substituted for the demand for justice.

Like Robinson Crusoe, Jane finds that prayer always meets a practical response, and the relationship of prayer and answer is an important thread in the action. She prays first for liberty but feels the prayer 'scattered on the wind', so—testifying to the discipline she tells us she has acquired —she substitutes the prayer for 'a new servitude' and thinks hard about ways and means. The answer is playfully dramatized as an internal colloquy, but in the full context of the novel there are other implications:

A kind fairy, in my absence, had surely dropped the required suggestion on my pillow; for as I lay down it came quietly and naturally to my mind: 'Those who want situations advertise; you must advertise in the *Herald*.' (ch. x)

The practical answers of Providence return in Jane's crisis. The vision recalls her painting of the Evening Star—

moonlit, vapourish, glorious-browed, shining in the blue—
and speaks to the spirit as the painted vision had been seen
by the spirit, saying, 'My daughter, flee temptation'. Later,
alone and hungry on the moor, re-enacting Bessie's hymn
which is an important source for feeling, image, and situation, she asks again, 'Oh, Providence, sustain me a little
longer! Aid—direct me!'. The 'false light' of the hymn
has been left behind, and what now appears as an *ignis
fatuus* is in fact the light of her cousin's house. As Kathleen
Tillotson notes in her analysis of the theme in *Novels of the
Eighteen-Forties*, coincidence is the symbol of Providence.
St John speaks to Jane when she has reconciled herself to
death and asserted her faith, 'Let me try to wait his will in
silence'. Finally her appealing prayer receives a direct
answer when she is tempted to accept her cousin's proposal
and is saved by hearing Rochester's voice. This is the conversation of her prayer and Rochester's, for his cry to her
has been the response to her prayer: 'Show me, show me
the path!' and her response to him has answered his prayer,
now that he has become capable of prayer like Crusoe, after
punishment and repentance.

> I asked of God, at once in anguish and humility, if I had not been
> long enough desolate, afflicted, tormented. . . . That I merited all I
> acknowledged—that I could scarcely endure more, I pleaded; and
> the alpha and omega of my heart's wishes broke involuntarily from
> my lips in the words 'Jane! Jane! Jane!' (ch. xxxvii)

It is only after Rochester too has been converted and has
repented that Providence can join their prayers as human
question and answer, and reconcile the human and the
divine, reason, conscience, and passion.

Kathleen Tillotson argues convincingly that Jane's converse with the invisible world gives the novel its moral unity
which makes us accept her decision as inevitable. This unity
is not entirely an individual one, but is rather imposed from
without, like the pattern of *Robinson Crusoe*. And the unity

of theme is only one aspect of unity. This is not to deny that the novel is animated and individual: Jane's conflict between discipline and passion for instance, before the great choice comes up, is delicately and plausibly dramatized in her defensive teasing and sparring, as well as being individualized and generalized in her relations with her aunt and cousins, and with her second set of cousins. To say that the novel is defined by an external doctrine is not to deny its realism, and we have only to compare it with stereotyped religious novels like those of Elizabeth Sewell or Charlotte Yonge, good enough of their kind, to see the superior subtlety of Charlotte Brontë's psychology and imagination. The moral pattern of the novel can be simply described, in terms of the conflict between human love and heavenly faith, passion and reason, rather as Mr Rochester's phrenological fortune-telling expresses it, as the conflict in which reason reins feeling, judgement overrules passions and desires, wind, earthquake and fire are succeeded by the still small voice of conscience. The psychological detail and personality of that conflict, within Jane and externalized in other characters, are not simply schematic. The Providential form allows for some free play of human relationships, both at their best, in Jane's own history and development, and at their weakest, in the traces of Angrian fantasy in Rochester's character and marriage and in the conclusion. There are places in the novel when this Providential form is a source not of unity but disintegration.

This weakness is by no means easy to pin-point, since it is a defect in belief rather than a straightforward literary lapse, though it is the literary consequences of belief which concern me most in this discussion. Both *Robinson Crusoe* and *Jane Eyre* are novels whose action relies on supernatural machinery and in each case it is not the artifice of fantasy but the fantasy of belief, which determines the movement and the motivation. In *Robinson Crusoe*, however, a much more persistently religious novel, there is no gap between realism and fantasy, and the fantastic explanation is merely one way of interpreting the material. Robinson Crusoe's dreams and voices appear at every crisis, but the crisis and its results are explicable in rational terms. When he dreams of rescuing a savage victim, it is a likely happening. When he decides not to hail the English longboat, he gives good reasons for not doing so. When he decides to travel by land from Portugal he is remembering past storms and shipwrecks. When he gives up the brewing project, it is explained as impracticable, because of the lack of yeast. It may be that the premise of the novel, his long survival in solitude, is explicable only in terms of his repentance and expiation, but this is the premise, scarcely to be challenged, and the handling of time and the constant sense of energetic reflection and activity give us no strained sense of plausibility. There are, moreover, the hysterical moments when the need for human company asserts itself wildly. Although the Providential form determines the action, there is a constant realistic explanation and accompaniment which makes it much more than religious fantasy.

In *Jane Eyre* the religious explanation determines motive and action in what is a more insistent and consistent fashion. And yet there is a gap in the novel which seems to be the result of its ideological pattern. This gap is one which may not be apparent to readers sharing Charlotte Brontë's beliefs, since they, like Charlotte Brontë, may be able to assume that faith is the product of growth and education. It is this assumption which allows the novelist to show two distinct stages in Jane's feelings and beliefs and leave the middle stage of transition undramatized. Yet it is a vital part of the novel's causality.

Jane is shown as passionate and intelligently rational. She begins with a need for love and self-respect and suffers aggression, rejection, and humiliation. Helen Burns puts her finger on Jane's 'excessive' need for human love and it is significant that Jane meets her friend's unquestioning faith with doubts and questions. When Helen confronts the sense of outrage with 'Love your enemies', Jane replies that this is impossible. When Helen on her death-bed affirms her faith and tells Jane, 'I am going to God', Jane asks, 'Where is God? What is God?' and, 'You are sure that there is such a place as heaven; and that our souls can get to it when we die?' She thinks to herself, 'Where is that region? Does it exist?'

We come to see that Jane achieves a rational discipline, and the tacit disappearance of her sense of outrage is acceptable enough as a consequence of maturity, especially since she has at Lowood found both affection and self-respect. We are not surprised when she forgives her aunt. This is an intelligible adult act of feeling which the child could not have achieved. What we do not come to see is exactly how Jane comes to accept Helen Burns's faith, even though such faith is at the root of her decision to leave Rochester. She has presumably moved away from her early doubts about Heaven by the time she comes to see her dying aunt, and her doubts are now of a different kind, about the actual destination of her aunt's spirit: 'Whither will that spirit—now struggling to quit its material tenement—flit when at length released?' There is an explicit reminder of Helen's death-bed, but our attention is not drawn to Jane's change in belief. She still speaks of *Helen's* beliefs. Her moment of affirmation comes with her moral crisis and test, not before it and she then affirms her need for dignity and self-respect, fully backed by the preceding action, and her faith that the 'invisible world' is impelling her towards the renunciation of Rochester. She has told us earlier that her love for Rochester 'stood between her and every thought of religion' but the actual growth of that religious feeling is the one thing the novel takes for granted and does not demonstrate. Every other detail in their courtship and conflict has roots which can be traced back to the beginnings. Her rejection of his extravagant gifts is entirely in keeping with her sense of dependence and memories of humiliation, and her hard-won independence and dignity comes out convincingly in her relations with the Ingrams, her wary pride as she keeps Rochester at a distance, and the characteristic flash, during her great moral conflict, when she remembers his cast-off mistresses and—prudently if unfairly—distrusts him. It is this pride and common sense which assert themselves at the time of choice. The religious argument is bound to be less convincing outside her faith just because Charlotte Brontë seems to have found it unnecessary to include religious development in the otherwise full and detailed account of Jane's growth. I am aware that her contemporary readers may have found it easier to share the undemonstrated assumption, but George Eliot's lack of moral sympathy with the novel, for instance, may well be explained by this incompleteness.

The question and answer of Jane's moral debate speaks in two voices, the voice of Christian law and the voice of personal prudence. Her love pleads for Rochester and indiscreetly flouts Jane's self-respect by asking, 'Who in the world cares for *you*? or who will be injured by what you do?' The answer is conventionally Christian in its content, but its tone is that of the child who complained so bitterly of injustice and humiliation, sharpened now by the experience of dignity and status, strengthened by rational detachment:

Still indomitable was the reply—'*I* care for myself. The more solitary, the more friendless, the more unsustained I am, the more I will respect myself. I will keep the order given by God; sanctioned by man.' (ch. xxvii)

Yet this is far from being a novel where we can ignore the religious references and observe only the psychological development. After Jane discovers that Rochester is already married she longs to die and there is only one sign of life: 'One idea only still throbbed lifelike within me—a remembrance of God.' We feel, I suggest, less that this one lifelike idea is the inevitable strength of a demonstrated faith, less that she would be violating a law which we have seen her learn in the course of her struggles, than that she is saved by the intervention of God.

It is true, as Kathleen Tillotson argues, that if Jane did not resist Rochester and the strong plea of love, 'the moral pattern of the novel would be violated'. I do not think, however, that the moral pattern is one which fully informs the dramatic psychology of the novel. In places it is taken for granted and not given proper emphasis. My distinction is perhaps plainer if we compare Jane's conflict and choice with that of Maggie Tulliver. Maggie rejects Stephen, and in most ways her position is easier than Jane's, since she would violate no actual divine or man-made *law* by marrying him. In other ways it is more difficult, since she faces injury to Lucy and Philip, whereas Jane is placed in the isolated position where she can hurt no one but herself. The distinction between breaking a commandment or a law, and hurting other people, is not the vital one here. There is the other important distinction, which I am trying to bring out, between an internally established and dramatized morality and an ideological assumption. Maggie acts and reasons in the clear context of her need for love and her ability to love, from her theoretical and untested self-abnegation. We feel that her motives are psychologically and morally unified, and whether we agree with her decision or not, there is no doubt about the moral continuity of the novel. Jane acts and reasons from precepts which have been presented strongly in Helen Burns, and much less emphatically in Jane herself. We have not seen the process of her religious education and faith, and the divine law which she invokes in the crisis has not been associated with either her feelings or her reason. Her choice comes from grace rather than from a continuity of moral and spiritual habit. The distinction is indicated by Charlotte Brontë herself, when Helen Burns tells Jane not to rely on her 'feeble self, or ... creatures feeble as you'. Robinson

Crusoe has to be checked in self-reliance and private enter-prise. George Eliot's characters have only their 'feeble selves' and their relationships with their fellows. Jane's *character* seems to demonstrate the strength of the individual and human relationships, but the *action* demonstrates the need for heavenly resources.

George Eliot rejected *Jane Eyre* not simply for the reason I have suggested, but also because she disapproved of the divorce laws, though she had not yet broken the command-ment Jane keeps: 'All self-sacrifice is good—but one would like it to be in a somewhat nobler cause than that of a diabolical law which chains a man soul and body to a putre-fying carcase' (*The George Eliot Letters*, ed. Gordon S. Haight, vol. i, p. 268). I do not think the weakness of the moral pattern lies in the nature of Jane's decision, or in Charlotte Brontë's silence on the subject of divorce law. Its weakness comes from imposing an ideology on to a realistic psychological pattern. The comparison with *Robinson Crusoe* should make it plain that I am using the word 'imposed' in a precise sense. Both novels show a belief in divine intercession and dramatize the workings of heavenly power and grace. I am not objecting to *Jane Eyre* because it expresses the belief that motivation is more than a personal and social matter but because it delineates faith in a rather muffled fashion. George Eliot shows action as determined by a mixture of social causes, moral and psychological habit, human influ-ence and chance. At some points she even suggests a Provi-dential cause, as in *Silas Marner* or at the end of *The Mill on the Floss*, but never within a moral conflict. Defoe and Charlotte Brontë make the Providential intervention crucial, both in action and conflict. *Robinson Crusoe* combines the hero's development with the ways of God in a way which has none of the strains of Charlotte Brontë's complex story, where the actual relations and conflict of Jane and Rochester could be seen quite independently of the Providential pat-tern, at least up to their parting. But the action depends

largely on that pattern, in its coincidences and its final outcome. The framework of the novel is consistently Providential, but within the frame there are omissions and
simplifications. I suggest that we should not hasten to
condemn Charlotte Brontë for writing out of neurotic
fantasy nor praise her for moral consistency and sound
psychology without examining the ways in which the ideology informs the novel as a whole.

It is the ideological assumption which makes it possible
for the fantasy to work, both in the destruction of Rochester
and in the happy ending. Whether or not we agree with
Richard Chase[1] that the dominant pattern is that of domesticated myth—'the tempo and energy of the universe can be
quelled, we see, by a patient, practical woman'—we should
surely observe the importance of the Providential form.
Chase observes that the universe is 'chastened by an assertion of will', and says that after the blinding of Rochester
'The universe, not previously amenable to supernatural
communication between the parted lovers, now allows them
to hear each other though they are leagues apart'. The
universe is acting in a coherent and consistent manner, for
it is Providence answering Rochester's prayer after confession and expiation. We may well observe that his actual
conversion is even less elaborated than Jane's, and once
again it is a pattern of action and change imposed from
without, grace rather than organic process, which determines and completes the story.

It may be thought that I am merely betraying impatience
with the simplicities of Christian dogma rather than describing some of their consequences, so I hasten at least to extend
my impatience to Hardy's pessimistic vision, which has the
very opposite metaphysical implications, but similar formal
results. In *Jude the Obscure* Hardy, like Charlotte Brontë,
succeeds in combining animated and realistic psychology
with ideological pattern. His story also depends on an

[1] See the interesting *Forms of Modern Fiction*, ed. W. Van O'Connor, p.109.

arrangement of action which reflects his general conclusions about the universe. This is the world without a Providence, where there is no malignant President of the Immortals, but conditions in nature and society which, in the absence of Providence, work together to frustrate energy and intelligence.[1] Those who best serve the life-force, like Arabella, prosper best, but those who have imagination and aspiration meet with the frustrations of nature's blind biological purpose and society's conventional restrictions. So 'nobody comes, because nobody does come', and Providence can be on occasion invoked with awful irony, because all is working towards frustration, not prosperity. At every point in his career Jude is checked: by his sexuality, by his poverty and class, by his love for and affinity with Sue. Her career ironically combines with his to make frustration definite: there is not only the fatal irony of their marriages, which overlap, but the irony of their ideological cross-purposes. Father Time is the symbolic short-cut which corresponds to Charlotte Brontë's Providential telepathy. This novel would surely be no different if Hardy had literally believed in a malignant supernatural improvidence. His 'crass casualty' imposes an energetic and external pattern as well as merely revealing itself in social and biological conditions. There is the same short-circuiting of internal and social determinism, though this shows itself unconvincingly only at one point, in the children's deaths, and on the whole does not lay an impossible implausibility on his materials.

There is another feature of ideological form, common both to the Providence novel and to Hardy's late novels, which is important. In the novels of Dickens, George Eliot, Meredith, and Tolstoy, free from this kind of metaphysical pattern, there is the constant play of opposites. If Romola progresses, Tito deteriorates, if Dorothea has a muted success, Lydgate has a failure, if Fred Vincy is redeemed,

[1] Those of us who share Hardy's metaphysical beliefs must still observe that Jude suffered from being born before the rise of the meritocracy.

Bulstrode is all but lost. A similar play of variations is present in Dickens and, most impressively and movingly, in Tolstoy. Life has a clear and schematic pattern, but it is like a game of snakes and ladders, at least in the presence of possibilities of success and failure, redemption and damnation, though not, like the game, in the pure environment of chance. Defoe and Charlotte Brontë choose a pattern where there are very few snakes. There are some characters in *Jane Eyre* who do not illustrate conscience and passion like Jane, Rochester, and St John Rivers, but there are no contrary examples illustrating the flouting of Providence unless we count John Reed and his mother who are too grossly foreshortened to act as proper counter-examples. Ideologically there is no reason why there shouldn't be. We are not asking for the kind of novel where the existence of Providence is both suggested and doubted, but merely for a novel where there are failures as well as successes, delineated in detail and substance within the author's ideological terms. We see what happens to those who flout Heaven in Robinson Crusoe's early career and in the case of Rochester, but the material is subdued to the optimistic selection, and here no doubt there are the pressures of wish-fulfilment as well as the pressures of strong belief. Defoe's interest in writing best-selling success stories and Charlotte Brontë's wish-fulfilment fantasy need not have conflicted with the Providential scheme. Commercial needs, private gratification, and ideology could co-operate to the one end, and are in any case perhaps not very easily separable as different causes, when we look at the actual novels.

It is even simpler in Hardy's late novels, for he has less possibility of acknowledging variation and exception. He is here writing from the belief that all worked for the worst. Although we can see him loading the dice, as when he chooses the ghastly examples of other marriages to warn and frighten Jude and Sue, this is scarcely even a distortion, according to his own terms. This game has all snakes and no ladders, and there are indeed moments when we feel that the strong statement of his vision leads to exaggeration or distortion, as in the multiplication of fatal coincidences in defiance of probability, or in the symbolic short-circuit. We can describe his moral pattern as one which excludes the possibility of another answer, or contrary evidence, but pessimism is by definition selective.

I do not think that this kind of dogmatically organized novel with its special features of single-track action and symbolic short-cuts is confined to the 'religious novel' written to a consistent belief, like the belief in Providence or the belief in the implications of an absent Providence. I should like therefore to end this chapter with the suggestion that the same kind of ideological form is to be found in a modern novelist, whose beliefs are not as easily codified as Defoe's or Charlotte Brontë's or Hardy's.

In *Aspects of the Novel* E. M. Forster has this to say about Hardy's novels:

> They are to be tragedies or tragi-comedies, they are to give out the sound of hammer-strokes as they proceed; in other words Hardy arranges the events with emphasis on causality, the ground plan is a plot, and the characters are ordered to acquiesce in its requirements. Except in the person of Tess (who conveys the feeling that she is greater than destiny) this aspect of his work is unsatisfactory. His characters are involved in various snares, they are finally bound hand and foot, there is ceaseless emphasis on fate, and yet, for all the sacrifices made to it, we never see the action as a living thing as we see it in *Antigone* or *Berenice* or *The Cherry Orchard*. The fate above us, not the fate working through us—that is what is eminent and memorable in the Wessex novels. (ch. v)

Although these and later remarks are compressed and sparsely illustrated, Forster appears to be saying about Hardy what might be said about his own novels. Most of them are written as ethical rather than metaphysical arguments, but they exhibit the same dogmatically imposed form which we find in the three novels I have just discussed.

We cannot say of them, it is true, that they are animated games of snakes or ladders, since with the exception of the most modest of them, *A Room with a View*, they are tentative and even ambivalent in their answers. They do provide answers, however, and these are answers to the plainly imposed question of the significance of human life. *Where Angels Fear to Tread* ends with the negation of action in Philip and Caroline, the two central characters, but though their vision cannot be translated into action, it is an affirmative vision. Philip finds the revelation of beauty and goodness when Caroline intervenes and saves him in his fight with Gino, and an even higher peak of revelation in her romantic love for Gino, which makes her renounce his own declaration of love. For Caroline, Gino represents her vision of romantic love and beauty.

The renunciations here may remind us of the end of *The Ambassadors*, the Providential voices of *Jane Eyre*, or even the symbolic deaths of the children in *Jude the Obscure*. They are symbolic acts rather than human demonstrations, and not altogether happy in their timing. After the brutal death of Gino's son, we find Philip's vision of the apotheosis of Caroline diverting us with its glamour where the action might seem to demand a moral climax in which these people recognized with horror and guilt and distress their responsibility and involvement. Instead we have aesthetic vision and, in each case, detachment from action. Even Caroline's love for Gino, despite its insistence on common sexual passion, is made with an inflated claim for maturity. She 'knows' that it will never die, which does not quite fit with the admission of its ordinary sexuality. 'Her experience has taught her', says Forster, but her experience has been consistently that of a spectator, even to her own passions, such as they are. Forster is anxious to illustrate his faith in beauty and human relationships, and his solution seems another interesting example of an ideological completion which may have settled the argument from the author's point of view but which is not substantiated. This completion is not only a glib one but introduces the wrong kind of discord.

Howards End and *A Passage to India* are also examples of novels which subordinate plausible action and psychology to an ideological pattern, but I do not wish to ventilate these matters at length since they are discussed by Frederick Crews, in his book, *E. M. Forster: The Perils of Humanism*, and argued in a detail more appropriate to a full-length study of Forster. I will give only a few examples of the ideological structure of these novels. The Providential symbolism of Mrs Wilcox, in *Howards End*, functions in much the same way as the figure of Father Time, though she is both a more central and a more shadowy figure. She is the symbol of tradition, a special kind of domesticated earth-goddess who is created by fantasy and made to intervene through fantastic machinery. She leaves the house to Margaret Schlegel, and though her family disregards her wish, Margaret becomes the mistress of Howards End. After death, she works through the agency of her familiar Miss Avery, who moves the Schlegel's furniture into the house and indirectly causes the breaking of Charles and Henry Wilcox. Mr Chase might see it, with some justification, as another instance of myth domesticated, with the repetition of Charlotte Brontë's motif of emasculation. Mrs Wilcox is the strongest source of hope for the threatened community, but her function throughout seems to be created by fantasy unbacked by moral action. It is true that the first thing we see her do is intervene with quiet tact after Helen's encounter with Paul, but this is a small instance of elementary common sense and sensibility and will hardly compensate for her passivity and vagueness in the rest of the novel. She silently devalues Margaret's intellectual friends when she comes to visit the sisters, but this can cut both ways for readers not wholly sympathetic to middle-class mother-figures. Her dramatic identity is mainly symbolic, unlike that of another image of heroic ordinariness,

Leopold Bloom. Bloom is also given symbolic generalization as a modern Ulysses and perhaps a Christ figure,
but he is still shown as an ordinary good man, and it is in
his moral acts and individual feelings that he provokes the
sympathy which makes ethical examples live. Mrs Wilcox
has much in common with Mrs Ramsay, in Virginia Woolf's
To the Lighthouse, yet another wife-and-mother figure who is
given an apotheosis not fully endorsed by what she says and
does. In *To the Lighthouse* we also meet again the Blooms-
bury evaluation of beauty, which gives Mrs Ramsay another
dimension which is stated but not dramatized. I cannot help
feeling that both Forster and Virginia Woolf overrate the
aesthetic qualities of human beings and relationships in a
way which Henry James, as aesthetic a *novelist* as either,
never did. James never creates inflated valuations of female
virtue and beauty which depend heavily on the reading of
striking moral significance into rudimentary hospitality and
basic maternal feeling. Both Mrs Wilcox and Mrs Ramsay
have a fatal resemblance to Mrs Dale and a significant lack
of resemblance to the Wife of Bath and Molly Bloom. Both
are interesting asexual portraits.

This is not just a matter of preferring sexual vitality and
lower-class mother love. In Mrs Moore in *A Passage to
India* Forster creates a character who also depends on
symbolic stature and fantastic action but whose virtues are
properly enacted, so that we respond not to an idea but to
an individual portrait. She is shown in action and change,
and Forster makes sparing use of the *ex officio* virtues of
maternity and no use at all of the aura of beauty. Mrs Moore
is convincingly detached and irritable in her relations with
her son Ronnie and Adela even before she goes into the
Marabar cave for her experience of vastation. She is given
something of the traditional aura of age but this is combined
with a realistic rendering of fatigue, techiness, and self-
centredness. Her wisdom is unmysterious good plain common sense. Her virtues are simply shown, beginning with

the humanity and courtesy she shows in the early encounter with Aziz at the mosque. If Leopold Bloom's virtue is compassion, also shown in action, Mrs Moore's is a consistent respect for other creatures, whether it is for the God of the mosque, for Aziz, whom she does not think of describing immediately as an Indian, or for the wasp. Both Bloom's compassion and Mrs Moore's respect may be called aspects of love. Mrs Moore loses her Christian feeling in the annihilating echo of the cave, and leaves Chandrapore in impatience and detachment, both characteristics developing consistently from what we have seen of her before. Both during her life and after it she, like Mrs Wilcox and Mrs Ramsay, is given a supernatural power: she identifies the ghost that causes the accident, and also tells Adela that it was not Aziz who was guilty, speaking on both occasions in an unconscious trance-like manner. But she is given the substance of moral action and vivid personality. The continuity of values in her two odd children is one of Forster's more successful codas, for they exist in her shadow, standing outside the world of doubt and common experience where Fielding, knowing that his wife knows more than he can understand, is separated from Aziz as their horses swerve apart in the last lines of the novel in the final image of frail human relationships.

Frederick Crews sees the novel as sceptical and pessimistic (chap. 10). He reminds us of Forster's 'disbelief in Providence' and suggests the sympathetic treatment of Hinduism is there in order to discredit the Christian and Moslem emphasis on personality: 'the vastness and confusion of India are unsuitable for an orderly, benevolent deity whose attention to individuals is tireless'. Hinduism, Islam, and Christianity, he concludes, are 'powerless before the nihilistic message of the Marabar Caves'. He seems to see this nihilistic message as final in its effects on Mrs Moore for he speaks of her adjusting 'her whole view of life to accord with the annihilation of value' and says that Adela, 'unlike Mrs

Moore . . . lacks the imagination to be permanently shattered by her irrational experience'. I find this implication
especially puzzling since Crews admits that the last words
of India to Mrs Moore—'So you thought an echo was
India; you took the Marabar Caves as final?'—affirm that
the Caves 'have not brought us into the presence of ultimate
truth'.

I suggest that Forster is pushing his intransigent material
as far as he can in the direction of optimistic hope. The anti-
vision is chiefly there, it seems to me, so that it shall be
powerfully withdrawn, both for Mrs Moore and for Adela.
Mrs Moore leaves Chandrapore and begins to revise her
anti-vision. She faces a landscape less melancholy than the
plain, and the houses built by man 'for himself and God'
strike her as 'indestructible' and 'appeared to her not in
terms of her own trouble but as things to see'. Instead of
wanting to leave she longs to stay, and stands looking in the
heat, fatally. She dies on leaving Bombay, after the rejection
of the echo.

Crews appears to overlook these aspects of the fantastic
machinery of the novel, perhaps because they are difficult to
reconcile with the pessimistic suggestions which he sees as
characteristic of Forster's last novel, perhaps because of their
muted tentativeness. When Mrs Moore's rejection of the
echo is swiftly followed by Adela's rejection and return to
sanity at the trial, we may wish to talk literally about Mrs
Moore's influence or metaphorically about her spirit. I
suggest that Forster is providing us with the possibility of a
miracle-working Mrs Moore, and that he prepares for this
earlier on when Mrs Moore suggests that the accident in the
car was caused by a ghost. Crews says at one point that
Forster is blocking off meaning from the reader as well as
from the characters, but this is not always true. He lets Mrs
Moore speak of the ghost, and then carefully tells the reader,
not the characters, that this fits the facts, showing us that it
is certainly how the Nawab Bahadur sees the incident. At

the end, when Godbole brackets Mrs Moore and the wasp, it is only the reader who has seen Mrs Moore bless the wasp. Forster is elsewhere so conscious of the uses of fantasy that it seems as if he wants to incorporate some supernatural suggestion. This is most important, and least definite, at the trial.

Forster is very careful to tell us exactly when Mrs Moore died, after leaving Bombay and before reaching Aden. Ronnie tells us at the trial that the boat should have reached Aden. This careful timetabling, taken in connection with the two pieces of supernatural evidence in the ghost and the wasp, suggests that Forster wishes to indicate the possibility of Mrs Moore transmitting her rejection of the Caves to Adela. She is made available for 'haunting' and the language used for Adela's new vision is at times religious. The vision commences when Mrs Moore is invoked, and when the chanting stopped, we are told 'It was as if the prayer had been heard, and the relics exhibited'. Adela's vision is not just the necessary vision of truth, but a total reversion, involving a vision of beauty. She is not restored to her old self but possessed by an experience which is temporary, though some of its effects are lasting: 'A new and unknown sensation protected her, like magnificent armour', 'smoothly the voice in the distance proceeded, leading along the paths of truth', 'something caused her to add', and 'though the vision was over, and she had returned to the insipidity of the world, she remembered what she had learnt. Atonement and confession—they could wait'. The language expresses a sense of protection and possession.

Later she thinks Fielding is speaking literally when he uses the word exorcism, and the talk turns to ghosts and Mrs Moore. They join in the 'fear' that the dead do not live again. This fear, and Fielding's later assertion of his disbelief in Providence, as against Hamidullah's belief, brings out the evidence plainly provided for the reader and also the evidence which is withheld from the characters.

I suggest that Forster deliberately builds up a supernatural status for Mrs Moore, and that even if we decide to reject a Providential interpretation of Adela's confession, the question is at least raised, and the possibility canvassed. The details of the ghost and the wasp are suggestions leaking through the crannies of realism. I do not think that Forster is smuggling in a Christian optimism, but that he is creating a sense of mystery which sets up obstacles to a sceptical reading. We may interpret the vision of Adela as the benevolent haunting of Mrs Moore which provides the main action with its solution. Mrs Moore's loving respect for individuals saves Aziz and Adela. The events which are mysterious or ambiguous suggest that love may be powerful, even if we do not go so far as to say that God is love. And the Hindu apotheosis is appropriate rather than ironical, or provides irony to criticize sects, not beliefs and visions. Forster revalues his humanism in a landscape and a society where the visions of beauty and love are obscure or hard to find, but he is still using symbolic short-cut and fantasy in order to make India more manageable, or at least to suggest possible grounds for faith in order. This is a much more complex ideological form than *Robinson Crusoe* or *Jane Eyre* but its schematic use of events and characters places it with them as a novel given shape by belief. Perhaps the pressure towards order is its weakness. A ghost's suggestion of hope or mystery is a fragile and whimsical use of the little gods in a novel about the great ones. So much of the material sustains the hardest look at the worst that this mystery seems manufactured, disrupting the truthfulness which is art's reflection of things as they are as well as being life's acceptance of things as they are. Moreover, the strength of Mrs Moore lies in her power of love, her respect for the individual, and the addition of a supernatural status seems a descent rather than an ascent. Nevertheless, even if we marvel at Forster's inability to resist fantasy, even in *A Passage to India*, the novel as a whole is larger and truer than its moments of convenient fantasy. And the fantasy itself makes its hints so gently that it can be overlooked.

I began by saying that an ethical pattern of belief can determine the form of the novel, and not always without distortion, as we may see in *Lady Chatterley*. Moral categories are common to most novelists, but a rigid religious dogmatism is not, and Georg Lukacs has gone so far as to suggest that the modern novel depends on secularized values and individual responsibility. Religious ideology imposes a special structure of beneficent action and directed character, and usually involves some dramatization of the invisible world which shapes itself in symbolism and fantasy. The religious novel need not dramatize Heaven. William Golding, even where he invokes the presence of God, as in *Pincher Martin*, is writing religious fables about the Fall, not about Providence, and his actual instances of sin are not specialized but recognizeable within most ethical codes. His action and characters are not ideologically distorted. The same is true of the better and later novels of Graham Greene, amongst which *The End of the Affair* stands out as an embarrassingly distorted Providence novel. Richardson's *Pamela* is a fascinating specimen which I have excluded as a Providence novel where the flaws are certainly not simply the product of the Providential pattern. The novels I have discussed have in common either a faith or a lack of faith which involves an active demonstration of a beneficent or metaphorically malignant intervention. Both action and dramatic psychology are accordingly limited. I should end by emphasizing once more that the form of these novels cannot be reductively equated with the form of their metaphysical fables, but that the pressure of ideology affects the form in certain common ways. The common formal features which I have isolated are the more marked because of the striking individual differences. Lawrence said that Hardy's 'form is execrable' because of 'his clumsy efforts to push events into line with his theory of being' but saw that 'his feeling, his instinct, his sensuous understanding' could fortunately work 'apart from his metaphysic' (*Phoenix*, ed. E. D. McDonald, p. 480). All the novelists I have taken to illustrate dogmatic form, attempt, with unfortunate results, to do what Lawrence calls applying the world to their metaphysic, but they are all happily incapable of doing this consistently. At times they apply the metaphysic to the world which breaks or enlarges the scheme and makes the novel more than a treatise or a fable.

CHAPTER IV

The Structure of Imagery:
George Meredith's *Harry Richmond*

T H E R E is one kind of fixed pattern I have not discussed or illustrated so far, and that is the pattern of recurrent imagery, whose clarity has by now been demonstrated by many critics, and whose function and nature have perhaps been necessarily exaggerated in the mere act of analysis. We are by now familiar, bored, and impatient with image analysis, well accustomed to the illustration of the unity and the argument by an extraction of related metaphors and similes and scenes. This method of extraction has of course the dangers of selectiveness: it is rather like scanning verse. 'The curfew tolls the knell of parting day' is probably as regular an iambic line as we can find, but the prosodic diagram of its stresses suggests an equality of beat and syllabic division which does violence to the actual sound of the line. Much of our work on narrative structure is as abstract. The skeletal scanning of narrative pattern cannot always discriminate between the weight of the individual units, because it is too unwieldy to combine the diagram of imagery with a detailed appreciation of the effect of each image, and because each repetition of theme depends not only on its content but on its place in the series, and that is something we can indicate but not measure. There are some novelists who do not suffer much outrage from this kind of diagrammatic selection. Henry James and Proust present the reader with a relatively neat and 'organic' serial pattern, and a bare diagram of the repeated motifs can give some idea of the nature of the novelist's preoccupation; where the novelist's imagination seems to aspire to unity and order, the critic can do some service in tracing that unity and order. But there are some novelists—Meredith is one—whose imagination seems at times to work in a less 'ordered' way, and a neat diagram of tracer elements in their scenes and metaphors could give a completely false impression.

Meredith uses repeated figures in his rhetoric, his scenes and his characters, and these figures are often correlatives of the theme. He also uses the correspondences which make images, scenes and characters co-operate in pointing a theme, and he relies on the running and changing structure in which a symbol carries the weight of related symbols or modifies some earlier statement. The context of his images sometimes carries the associations of traditional and 'natural' symbols, so that the symbolism of the novel is partly external, partly particularized and locally manufactured within the novel. Meredith differs from most of the novelists whose patterns I have analysed in his greater degree of discordance and casualness. In many of his novels, and very strikingly in *The Adventures of Harry Richmond*, there is a large area of freedom which surrounds the serial structure. Most novels which have any realism and particularity must have this kind of freedom. The language and characterization cannot be entirely committed to generalizing the theme, or to reminding us of it. Total relevance is rarely found outside James. The truthfulness and readability of fiction depends on characters and language acting in the interest of local vitality as well as in the interest of overriding theme. What sets Meredith apart from those novelists whom he superficially resembles, is the freedom and casualness of scenes and rhetoric which do have an apparent connection with the thematic stream. It is as if *The Golden Bowl* contained imagery coloured by the central figure of the bowl but, having no moral commentary to offer, insisted on displacing the series instead of taking its place in it.

In order to show the way in which Meredith breaks his pattern, and dissolves his view, I must first treat him as if he were Henry James, and offer some account of the pattern. *The Adventures of Harry Richmond* is a *Bildungsroman*, superficially episodic in form, and its theme is the education of Harry, to whom, as to King Lear and Catherine Morland, 'the real world grew visible'. It is also—in a sense—an anti-Providence novel. Harry's progress is presented in counterpoint against the career of Richmond Roy, at first his familiar and double, ultimately his opposite. The two characters move together in a striking account of father shaping son and son growing away from father. We are given two versions of romantic egoism—the egoism which can be taught to know its place, and the egoism which is 'the unteachable spirit' of Richmond Roy.

Meredith's tone is so sophisticated that he can manipulate violent and marvellous material without ever touching the rawness and improbability of melodrama, and Harry's spectacular 'adventures' are all steps in his moral progress, accompanied by images and analogies which often underline their moral function. But the dazzle of Harry's enchantments, which are in the end revalued or lost enchantments, is also the direct poetic portrayal of his sensibility: the excitement of the early pastoral scenes, or 'The Great Fog and the Fire at Midnight', or 'The Statue on the Promontory', or the burning of Riversley, or the brilliant dream-fragments is primarily the excitement of romantic vision, and not the excitement of event. Our main interest in this first-person narrative lies in the nature and change of Harry's imagination, in part a special case, fostered by special illusions, but basically the common human loss of young wonder.

The big scenes in this novel have a symbolic function: they demonstrate sensibility and action, they often have their natural or 'archetypal' associations, and they are sometimes left to work obliquely on Harry. The effect of these scenes is often reinforced by duplication and coincidence, and is also accompanied by a cluster of satellites in the imagery. Sometimes the symbol relies chiefly on imagery, is never solidified or expanded into dramatic enactment.

The most prominent images are present both in scene and in the accompanying rhetoric. Captain Jasper Welsh, after kidnapping Harry and Temple in order to save their souls on board his barque, the *Priscilla*, tells them: 'I pray for no storm, but, by the Lord's mercy, for a way to your hearts through fire or water' (ch. xiii)—a prophetic wish which comes true and extends beyond the salvation of Harry Richmond. Fire and water are recurring figures, and we have air and earth thrown in for good measure, though it would be inadvisable to make of this novel an allegory of the Four Elements. (These images are closely related to images used variously in Meredith's poetry, but the relationship can only be mentioned here.)

The scenes run into each other, and their relationship is as unpredictable as their content. Harry—not for the first time or the last—runs away to find his father. He is led through baffling fog to heroic fire, where he and Temple help in the rescue while a woman they have met in the crowd looks after Harry's watch and gives the mate of the *Priscilla* the impression that the boys are in need of moral rescue. But the voyage of the *Priscilla* and a chance meeting with Clara Goodwin, the 'Peribanou' of Harry's childhood travels, leads him to his father after all. The voyage, like most of the other events in the novel, is interpreted by Harry as the guiding of his special Providence, and it is not until the end of the novel that his view of Providence, an echo of his father's, is put in its place. This voyage stands out as a stage in Harry's moral progress, taking its colour from Captain Welsh, an unequivocal representative of truth in a book where truth has many faces. Captain Welsh mistakes the immediate occasion for rescue from the dangerous navigation of that sea-born Venus whose guidance 'leads to the bottom beneath us'. Harry is innocent on this occasion, but the rescue is proleptic, and his later amorous career points back to the relevance of Captain Welsh's fears. The episode is thrown into relief by coincidence and analogue: Captain Welsh tells the boys how his brother was drowned in the Pool of London with his sweetheart and the drunken 'young University gentleman' who had seduced her, and both the kidnapping of Harry and Temple and the Captain's story come to life at the end when once more the *Priscilla* sails on a moral mission, with Harry's childhood sweetheart and another drunken young university gentleman who had seduced *her*. Captain Welsh is to take Mabel Sweetwinter, 'beautiful as Solomon's bride' and 'as weak as water', and predicts: 'she shall know the mercy of the Lord on high seas' (ch. iv). Edbury, who has seduced Mabel, goes to find her and is kidnapped just as Harry and Temple were, and the *Priscilla* meets its storm, bringing back to mind Temple's first prophecy:

Don't you remember my saying the Priscilla was the kind of name of a vessel that would go down with all hands, and leave a bottle to float to shore? A gin-bottle was found on our East coast—the old captain must have discovered in the last moments that such things were on board—and in it there was a paper . . . '*The Lord's will is about to be done*'; and underneath—'*We go to his judgment resigned and cheerful*'. (ch. lvi)

It also takes us back to Captain Welsh's words to Temple when the boy laughs at his preaching, 'I'll meet you in leviathan's mouth on the night of a storm' (ch. xiii). Here the symbolism of sea and storm is inseparable from all that is condensed in the character of the old Captain, who accepts no compromise and goes back to sea rather than accept his doubtful victory in the lawsuit—incidentally making Temple admit his responsibility for that decision and his death, and thus involving Temple in the last storm after all. Captain Welsh, Richmond Roy's opposite, is 'clad in armour proof against earthly calamity'; it is he who carries the burden of the 'lost souls' and provides a nemesis for some characters and a release for others. Not only is the voyage repeated: once more Harry interprets events in the egoistic light of a special Providence. Harry is also at sea in the storm that wrecks the *Priscilla*: 'At night it blew a gale. I could imagine it to have been sent providentially to brush the torture of the land from my mind, and make me feel that men are trifles' (ch. lvi). Later, knowing what the storm has done for him, he thinks, 'An odd series of accidents' (ibid.). The measure of his progress is taken when he comes to reject the Providential interpretation his father has preached both for himself and his son:

> I was still subject to the relapses of a not perfectly right nature, as I perceived when glancing back at my thought of 'An odd series of accidents!' which was but a disguised fashion of attributing to Providence the particular concern in my fortunes: an impiety and a folly! This is the temptation of those who are rescued and made happy by circumstances. The wretched think themselves spited, and are merely childish, not egregious in egoism. (ibid.)

When Harry rejects the Providence of his father's Podsnappian faith ('I am watched over', 'power placed in my hands by Providence', 'I was under heaven's special protection', and so on) it is to see the part played in his 'Providence' by human beings. Ottilia has been his Providence as Dorothy, fatally, was his father's—and he comes to admit that if Providence may be thanked, it is not proudly, but humbly, as Captain Welsh accepts his Providence. Sea and storm play their part in Harry's true and false Providence, and the Captain Welsh episodes are presented with complete explicitness. We are not even permitted to let the repetition make the emphasis for us, but have our attention drawn to 'the sedate practical irony'. Not that Meredith draws all his strands together quite so explicitly; he lets us observe for ourselves the fulfilment of Captain Welsh's wish that Harry's heart should be won by fire and water.

The sea-adventures have their constellation of metaphor. Some are plainly coloured by the fatal shipwreck:

He dreamed he was in a ship of cinammon-wood upon a sea that rolled mighty, but smooth immense broad waves, and tore thing from thing without a sound or a hurt. (ch. i)

The city that would some night or other vanish suddenly, leaving bare sea-ripple to say 'Where? where?' as they rolled over. (ch. iv)

My dreams led me wandering with a ship's diver under the sea, where we walked in a light of pearls and exploded old wrecks. I was assuring the glassy man that it was almost as clear beneath the waves as above, when I awoke to see my father standing over me in day-light; and in an ecstasy I burst into sobs. (ch. xviii)

Such faith had the quiet, thoughtful young man at Riversley in the convulsions of the future, the whirlwinds and whirlpools spinning for him and all connected with him, that he did not object to hear his name and Janet's coupled, though he had not a spark of love for her. (ch. xxiii)

He had so saturated himself with the resources, evasions and des-perate cruising of these light creatures of wind, tide, and tempest. . . . (ch. xlv)

These images are—more or less—connected with the power of sea and shipwreck, and some are anticipations or echoes of real events. This is where classification by the con-tent of imagery breaks down.[1] To begin with, the first three examples given above are not important *because* they form part of an image-series. They belong to another series too, and assert its life most strongly: the life of Harry's dreams and fantasy. The first and third examples are taken from actual dreaming, the first shaped as a dream of sea by the rhythm of Harry's sleep in his father's arms on the midnight walk, the third a brilliant fragmentary shuffle of the incident of the Statue—his father was enclosed, like the diver, and

[1] I must make it plain that I have not attempted to give more than a selection from the various image-series in the novel.

the Shakespearean overtones remind us briefly of another
father and son. The second is a bit of childish excited fantasy. All make their contribution to the life of excited wonder
which is Harry's susceptibility to his father's potent charm
and a strongly assertive piece of charm for the reader. Their
place in the thematic chain may be noted, but should not be
dwelt on. Moreover, there is another set of related images—
related again if we are classifying by content. Our attention
is drawn to them by a chapter-title, 'I am Carried by the
Tide'.

Dr Julius Karsteg says to Harry, 'Then I apprehend that
you wait for the shifting of the tide to carry you on?' (ch.
xxix), and this is later taken up in a series of images used by
Richmond Roy: 'I am taking the tide, Richie'; 'The tide
took me . . .'; 'You will find me in full sail on the tide';
'We are in the very tide of success'; and 'so I was carried
on the tide with him' (ch. xxxix). This throws up several
other images, including: 'The heavy slip of her tongue that
threw us into heavy seas when we thought ourselves floating
in canal waters' (ch. xxxviii); and 'I pilot you into harbour,
and all you can do, is just the creaking of the vessel to me'
(ch. l); and 'The image of Ottilia conjured up pictures of a
sea of shipwrecks, a scene of immeasurable hopelessness'
(ch. xliv). There may be some overlapping, as in the last
image, which is connected with Richmond Roy's scheming
and with the more 'organic' and poetically presented
imagery of wreck, but these and other examples of the
related image have on the whole a different effect from those
I have quoted before. They have their source in Richmond
Roy's highly artificial and repetitive rhetoric, and, like most
of his metaphors, are only rather grandly flourished clichés.
We *might* argue an ironical distinction between these fanciful
images of Roy's characteristic style, and the deeper-rooted
emotionally presented images which seem to be more
organically connected with the central symbols; but I suspect that this would be over-ingenious. The relationship of

the content is, I think, overridden by the sharp indifference in tone and treatment.

There is yet another series of sea-images, distinguished by having their source within the novel. Harry says of Ottilia that she was imaged for him by 'the controlled sea-deeps', and this is connected less with the shipwreck imagery than with the ecstatic sea-scenes where Ottilia sails in Harry's yacht—an amorous correlative very like the swimming scene in *Lord Ormont and his Aminta*. (The sea as amorous image runs throughout Meredith.) There is a small anticipation when Harry's father speaks of the day when 'I should be a legal man, embarked in my own ship' (ch. iv). In the chapter, 'On Board a Yacht' the occasion engenders its own local images:

> Just taking impressions as they came, like the sands in the ebb-tide.

> No cloud on sun and moon. We had gold and silver in our track, like the believable children of fairyland.

Ottilia is also associated with scenes by the lake near her palace, and at the end with an English sea:

> I came on the smell of salt air, and had that other spirit of woman around me, of whom the controlled sea-deeps were an image, who spoke to my soul like starlight. (ch. l)

The actual sea-scapes connected with the love of Harry and Ottilia also take on the excitement of her childish romantic admiration of the English sea-heroes and England's 'ancient grandeur': 'our souls were caught together on the sea' (ch. xxxi). The sea and sunset images springing out of Harry's sailing with Ottilia, however, resist a neat pigeon-holing. Harry moves from his memory of 'the desolate days before I saw her wheeled in her invalid chair along the sands and my life knew sunrise' to his English associations, to home, and to Janet:

> But whatever the mood of our affections, so it is with us island wanderers: we cannot gaze over at England, knowing the old country

to be close under the sea-line, and not hail it, and partly forget ourselves in the time that was. The smell of sea-air made me long for the
white cliffs, the sight of the white cliffs revived pleasant thoughts of
Riversley, and thoughts of Riversley thoughts of Janet, which were
singularly and refreshingly free from self-accusations. (ch. xxxvi)

Here a reason for the shift in imagery is the ambivalence
of Harry's love. Meredith's imagery moves out of its
apparently fixed pattern in many places and for many
reasons. There is no single centre in scene and action from
which a trail of thematic imagery emerges. There are several
sources, and the imagery from each crosses and overlaps and
confuses classification.

'A way to your hearts through fire and water': fire too
has its part to play in the novel. The scenes of fire are, with
an important exception, associated with Richmond Roy.
When he rouses Riversley in the first chapter, the clamour
of the bell is woven into the Squire's dream:

At the first touch the Squire sprang up, swearing by his Lord Harry
he had just dreamed of fire, and muttering of buckets. 'Sewis! you're
the man, are you: where has it broken out?' 'No, sir; no fire,' said
Sewis; 'you be cool, sir.' 'Cool, sir! confound it, Sewis, haven't I
heard a whole town of steeples at work?'

This is only a dream of fire, but Richmond Roy does
start a real fire at midnight, in the lake-palace library, and
the close reader will find some recapitulation in the second
scene of ringing bells and servants' clamour. Richmond Roy
seizes Ottilia's silver lamp and sets fire to the curtains in an
attempt to cover the secret meeting of the lovers. The act is
set in character. 'Incendiary', shrieks Baroness Turckems,
and Harry has two significant comments:

And I had, I must confess, a touch of fear of a man who could
unhesitatingly go to extremities as he had done, by summoning fire
to the rescue. (ch. xxxvi)

Me the whole scene affected as if it had burnt my skin. I loathed that
picture of him, constantly present to me, of his shivering the glass of

Ottilia's semi-classical night-lamp, gravely asking her pardon, and stretching the flame to the curtain, with large eyes blazing on the baroness. The stupid burlesque majesty of it was unendurable to thought. (ibid.)

'As if it had burnt my skin', 'with large eyes blazing'—it will be observed that the scene has already begun to spawn its local metaphors which reinforce the symbolic interpretations of the event. Repetition does much to elevate event into symbol. The novel ends where it begins, at Riversley and at night, and this time the squire's dream of fire has been lit by Richmond Roy's grandiose and irresponsible violence, though this is the violence of his crazy old age, not the cool scheming sanity of the man who applied Ottilia's lamp to the curtains. Harry and Janet have just come back to England:

We saw the dark sky ominously reddened over Riversley, and, mounting the ridge, had the funeral flames of the old Grange dashed in our faces. The blow was evil, sudden, unaccountable. . . . The Grange was burning in two great wings, that soared in flame-tips and columns of crimson smoke, leaving the central hall and chambers untouched as yet, but alive inside with mysterious ranges of lights, now curtained, now made bare—a feeble contrast to the savage blaze to right and left, save for the wonder aroused as to its significance. These were soon cloaked. Dead sable reigned in them, and at once a jet of flame gave the whole vast building to destruction. My wife thrust her hand in mine. Fire at the heart, fire at the wings—our old home stood in that majesty of horror which freezes the old limbs of men, bidding them look and no more. (ch. lvi)

We gathered that a great reception had been prepared for us by my father: lamps, lights in all the rooms, torches in the halls, illuminations along the windows, stores of fireworks, such a display as only he could have dreamed of. (ibid.)

The event has the full naturalistic status of event placed plausibly in character, but the coincidental link with the earlier fire makes it stand out as symbol.[1] The aggressive

---

[1] Compare the fires in *Jane Eyre*, to which *Harry Richmond* doubtless owes something.

magician has made one more transformation scene. But he is burnt in his own fire, looking for Dorothy. The heroic touch is toughened by his futility; he should have known that Dorothy was not there. We are left with the redeeming feature, even though it is underplayed, that his heart was not 'brazen'. He topples from the bronze horse when he sees his son, he dissuades Harry from seducing Mabel Sweetwinter, he once saved the honour of the Marquess of Edbury, and in his curious literal fashion he has preserved a kind of fidelity to Dorothy. Violence, grandiose futility, and heroics, are all blended in this last scene.

Like water, fire is given its big scenes and their satellite images. It would be possible to select judiciously and suggest a coherent symbolic pattern. Fire-images accompany Roy's progress. When his grand series of balls is announced, the Squire says:

> Hark you, Mr. Harry; dance your hardest up in town with your rips and reps, and the lot of ye; all very fine while the burning goes on: you won't see the fun of dancing on the ashes. A nice king of Rome Nero was next morning! (ch. xli)

This casual scornful association stands out because it has a place in the series—or rather in two series, because it is not only a fire-image but also one of the pervasive images of royalty. It is also oblique prophesy. When the Squire calls Roy a 'fireship', it unites two motifs. Then there is the image which fixes Harry's despair when he is on his way to see Ottilia, and passes Riversley: 'I passed the Riversley station under sombre sunset fires, saddened by the fancy that my old home and vivacious Janet were ashes, past hope' (ch. l). This is linked also with the pervasive image of sunset, associated with the German forest, the sea-meeting with Ottilia, and the sunset, mistaken for sunrise, on board the *Priscilla*. On the next page Harry sees his father, in the light of Ottilia's calm vision, as 'an *ignis-fatuus*'.[1]

---

[1] Another important image in *Jane Eyre*.

But there are other fire-images which read out of series, though it might be claimed that they question the established pattern rather than blur it. Meredith enlivens several common enough metaphors of fire: there is the 'inner fire' of Ottilia, the senses taking fire, Janet's comment on a famous Admiral, 'Kindling our blood like a beacon', and in the last chapter, clustered assertively around the final symbol, some of these half-dead metaphors are dwelt on strongly:

The signs unfamiliar about her for me were marks of the fire she had come out of; the struggle, the torture, the determined sacrifice, through pride's conception of duty. She was iron once. She had come out of the fire finest steel.

I know that this possession of hers, [courage] which identifies her and marks her from the rest of us, would bear the ordeal of fire.

Immediately, the metaphors are tested by the event. Once more the non-literal nature of imagery insists that the related scene should also move beyond a strictly literal life. There is a sinister jump from names to facts—rather like saying 'Come in' to an anonymous knock, and inviting the Devil. The images do not remain as images. They act as invitation and prelude to the real fire—metaphor is acted out in immediate coincidence. The half-dead image of trial by fire is given real flames. The images present the fire as ordeal and heroism, not merely for Janet and Harry, though it has been prophesied of both that they may be tried by fire, but also for Richmond Roy. The image points in another direction and the symbol becomes ambivalent, as indeed fire is, traditionally and naturally, both destructive and potent, presenting hell, purgatory, and Prometheus.

This of course is still a schematic interpretation, and it may be that I am exaggerating the connectedness of these images. Certainly there is one scene of fire which stands outside both series, the purgatorial symbols and the destructive ones. This is the Great Fire in London, one of the strange events in the chain which brings Harry, by fog,

fire, and flood, to his father. Like the fog, it is a transformation scene. The external event is lit by Harry's imagination.
Harry and Temple wander in the fog. They meet a man who
grasps Temple's shoulders, groaning, 'My son! I've lost
my son', as Harry searches for his father. The boys have
already thought of themselves as Apollo and Mercury,
Harry of himself as Telemachus, and the fire is presented as
a heroic dream:

The firemen were on the roofs of the houses, handsome as Greek
heroes, and it really did look as if they were engaged in slaying an
enormous dragon, that hissed and tongued at them, and writhed its
tail, paddling its broken big red wings in the pit of wreck and smoke,
twisting and darkening—something fine to conquer, I felt with
Temple. (ch. xi)

Here the fire has little to do with ordeal or aggression: it
is the splendid excitement of fire, another wild adventure
for Harry Richmond, coloured by his romantic sensibility.
But the repetition of scenes of fire inevitably draws attention
to this scene, apparently linked only casually with the main
stream. In this novel many adventures are repeated: there
are two voyages of the *Priscilla*, with moral captives aboard;
Harry is twice 'rescued' by Kiomi and twice wakes on her
breast; there are two fights, and each is exploited by Richmond Roy, who falsely summons Ottilia to Harry's sick bed,
and twice she comes. The habit of repetition, not always
reinforcing symbol, does something to explain the odd
appearance of scenes and images linked by content but not
by 'meaning'.

There are images of earth and air, often presented in
antithesis:

I found myself shooting down from the heights of a dream among
shattered fragments of my cloud-palace before I well knew that I had
left off treading common earth. (ch. xxvi)

Some love for my home, similar to what one may have for Winter,
came across me, and some appreciation of Janet as well, in whose

society I was sure to be at least myself, a creature much reduced in altitude, but without the cramped sensations of a man on a monument. My hearty Janet! I thanked her then for seeing me of my natural height. (ch. xxxvi)

Janet is 'a green field of the springs' passed by 'a climber up the crags' (ch. xliv) as Harry aspires to Ottilia's height, and this imagery takes its force from the contrast of the two women and the two countries: 'I thought of Janet—she made me gasp for air; of Ottilia, and she made me long for earth' (ch. l).

The contrast is also that between Harry and Ottilia: he is usurping her element, and pulling her down: 'I thought neither of winning her, nor of aiming to win her, but of a foothold on the heights she gazed at reverently' (ch. xxx), but after he has in fact tried to win her, he thinks of her as 'dropping from a height' when the 'senses took fire', and this itself echoes an earlier parting when he sees her as 'a bird about to fly' and returning 'to the upper world' (ch. xxxi). There are many instances of this kind of insistence:

'Rather the extremes!—I would rather grasp the limits of life and be swung to the pits below, be the most unfortunate of human beings, than never to have aimed at a star. You laugh at me? An Englishman must be horribly in earnest to talk like as I do now. But it is a star!' (The image of Ottilia sprang fountain-like into blue night heavens before my eyes memorably.) (ch. xxix)

She raised me to learn how little of fretful thirst and its reputed voracity remains with love when it has been met midway in air by a winged mate able to sustain, unable to descend farther. (ch. xxxv)

I went from the room and the house, feeling that I had seen and heard her who was barely of the world of human-kind for me, so strongly did imagination fly with her. (ch. xlviii)

Ottilia is infected by such images, but not to the extent of becoming conceptualized into a symbol of romantic aspirations: imagination flies with her, and she is 'a touch-stone, a relentless mirror, a piercing eye, a mind severe as

the Goddess of the God's head ... a remorseless intellect';
'She was truth' (ch. xlviii), and later, 'my providence', but
this is kept human. It is her uncompromising, though com-
promised, intelligence, and not her rank, which gives her
stature, even though we are bound to feel a little unhappy
about the presentation of her republican theories. Harry's
failure to reach her height is more convincing in its moral
than in its social implications, and it is a human failure carefully prepared in terms which give warmth and not con-
descension to his return to Janet. When Captain Welsh
holds up to Harry and Temple the stern mirror of the
Prodigal Son, it displaces the more flattering mirror of
Telemachus:

> We talked of Ulysses and Penelope. Temple blamed him for leaving
> Calypso. I thought Ulysses was right, otherwise we should have had
> no slaying of the Suitors: but Temple shyly urged that to have a
> Goddess caring for you (and she was handsomer than Penelope, who
> must have been an oldish woman) was something to make you feel as
> you do on a hunting morning, when there are half-a-dozen riding-
> habits speckling the field—a whole glorious day of your own among
> them! This view appeared to me very captivating, save for an obstruc-
> tion in my mind, which was, that Goddesses were always conceived
> by me as statues. They talked and moved, it was true, but the touch of
> them was marble; and they smiled and frowned, but they had no
> variety: they were never warm. (ch. xi)

Harry leaves a Calypso for a Penelope—though only in a
restricted sense. These are scarcely parallels, merely temporary analogies: Ottilia is no Calypso, but attached tenuously to the Calypso-Penelope antithesis via the image of
goddess and statue; Janet, who keeps her suitors in play by
devious means, and who is there for Harry to come home to,
is closer to Penelope; Harry is both Telemachus (ironically,
like Stephen Dedalus in a later analogy) and Ulysses. The
analogy fits temporarily, is dropped, or used again with a
difference.

The most important statue in *Harry Richmond* is the

impersonated statue of bronze, and with it goes a series of images and suggestions linked in content but not in moral association with the images of height and statue describing Ottilia. The statue is on a height beside the lake-palace, faintly recalling the image Harry uses of his memory of the night his father carried him off:

> That night stands up without any clear traces about it or near it, like the brazen castle of romance round which the sea-tide flows. (ch. ii)

The statue scene is the literal enactment of so much in Richmond Roy: mountebank, romantic, noble in appearance, unrealistic and false in aspiration. The statue becomes a symbol of the man:

> And the statue was superb—horse and rider in new bronze polished by sunlight.

> 'It is life-like; it is really noble! it is a true Prince!'

and

> No Prince Eugene—nay, nor Marlborough, had such a martial figure, such an animated high old warrior's visage. (ch. xvi)

It is no static objective correlative for Richmond Roy's desire, but shifts its emphasis like James's golden bowl. It is both Roy's weakness and his touch of nobility. He topples, and he plays Falstaff unnecessarily, multiplying his minutes of endurance with the craziness of the incorrigible liar, but he topples because he sees his son, for his heart is not 'brazen', and when later the real statue of the royal prince is made it looks less noble than Roy. The scene, like Roy's carefully manipulated rhetoric, marks the delicate poise which he maintains almost until the end, the poise between dignity and grotesque inflation. It is an image eminently reconcilable with Harry's dream of hunting his father 'in an unknown country, generally with the sun setting before me' (ch. v). The excited landscape of this dream is matched by the event. The distance between the statue scene and the revolting humiliation of a later scene when the false Dauphin shows his birthmark (emphasized as it is by being told several times, once in gross parody) marks the step Harry has taken towards his necessary disenchantment.

Images of height accompany the echoes of the statue scene—unlike Ottilia's loftiness, this is height which cannot be reached or, if reached, cannot be sustained. Richmond Roy tells Harry: ' . . . My grandest edifices fall; there is no foundation for them' (ch. xix), and Harry catches the infection of the image, without seeing through it. In the next paragraph he says, 'I was so full of my sense of triumph in my adventurous journey and the recovery of my father, that I gazed on the old Grange from a towering height'.

When his progress is marked by doubts of his father, the image is revalued—here it recollects the fall from the statue:

> I know nothing to equal the anguish of an examination of the basis of one's pride that discovers it not solidly fixed; an imposing cellarage. . . . Whether in the middle of life it is advisable to descend the pedestal altogether, I dare not say. Few take the precaution to build a flight of steps inside—it is not a labour to be proud of; fewer like to let themselves down in the public eye—it amounts to a castigation; you must, I fear, remain up there, and accept your chance in toppling over. (ch. xxxiii)

Another aspect of the statue motif is picked up when Harry, having said that Janet saw him 'of his natural height', adds, 'I lay down to sleep in my old home, feeling as if I had thrown off a coat of armour' (ch. xxxvi). There are of course more unmistakable echoes, as when Roy returns thanks 'on behalf of an Estate of the Realm' and Harry thinks, 'It led him to perform once more as a Statue of Bronze before the whole of gaping London!' (ch. xlii).

There are two images of the statue, the Goddess and the impersonated Royalty, and two images of height, the true and the false. Harry is educated by true height to reject the false, and his coming to earth in Janet (circumstantial though it is) is given some implication of true moral choice by his rejection of all—or almost all—that his father stands for. He comes to accept what Dr Julius tells him and finds his true element: 'It's that light dancer, that gambler, the heart in you . . . which aims itself at inaccessible heights, and has the fall.' But it is in fact solid earth, and not 'a handful of dust' (Karsteg's phrase) which remains for him at the end.

Imagery is presented in a moving chain, and the chain sometimes breaks, either revealing an ambivalence or contradiction which is more than merely rhetorical, which may correspond to a moral or psychological knot, or in order to make separate and independent local impressions. Henry James's concentrated form has an unusually sustained major reference, contrasting with the more graduated pattern of the expansive novel, where many details exist for the sake of local rather than central effect, and Meredith's pattern of imagery gives us interesting examples of this kind of detail. He uses imagery not merely in order to mark a wayward moral progress, but in order to define, with strong local gleams, the sensations of his hero. He gives full play, for instance, to the ecstatic vision of childhood, which is to be subdued by sober experience. Its glamour is seen as illusory, though not always spurious, and the charm of this novel—surely Meredith at his most readable—springs largely from the direct expression of the genuine though temporary flamboyance of the child's wonder, natural, limited, and nostalgically regretted. There is a series of dazzling images, sometimes linked with the symbolic pattern, primarily interesting in their own right:

It appeared to him that the stranger was of enormous size, like the giants of fairy books: for as he stood a little out of the doorway there was a peep of night sky and trees behind him, and the trees looked very much smaller, and hardly any sky was to be seen except over his shoulders. (ch. i)

He had the world beyond the hills; I this one, where a slow full river flowed from the sounding mill under our garden wall, through long meadows. In winter the wild ducks made letters of the alphabet flying. (ch. iii)

She showed me a beautiful little pink bed, having a crown over it, in a room opening to my father's. Twenty thousand magnificent dreams seemed to flash their golden doors when I knew that the bed was mine. . . . (ch. iv)

Then it was that I could think earnestly of Prince Ahmed and the kind and beautiful Peribanou, whom I would not have minded his marrying. My favourite dream was to see him shooting an arrow in a match for a prize, and losing the prize because of not finding his arrow, and wondering where the arrow had flown to, and wandering after it till he passed out of green fields to grassy rocks, and to a stony desert, where at last he found his arrow at an enormous distance from the shooting line, and there was the desert all about him, and the sweetest fairy ever imagined going to show herself in the ground under his feet. . . . (ch. iv)

During this Arabian life, we sat on a carpet that flew to the Continent, where I fell sick, and was cured by smelling at an apple. . . . (ibid.)

Temple did not think it strange that we should be riding out in an unknown world with only a little ring, half a stone's-throw clear around us, and blots of copse, and queer vanishing cottages, and larches and birches rigged like fairy ships, all starting up to us as we passed, and melting instantly. One could have fancied the fir trees black torches. (ch. x)

Not being able, however, to imagine the Bench a happy place, I corrected the excess of brightness and gave its walls a pine-torch glow; I set them in the middle of a great square and hung the standard of England drooping over them in a sort of mournful family pride. Then, because I next conceived it a foreign kind of place, different altogether from that home growth of ours, the Tower of London, I topped it with a multitude of domes of pumpkin or turban shape, resembling the Kremlin of Moscow, which had once leapt up in the eye of Winter, glowing like a million pine-torches, and flung shadows of stretching red horses on the black smoke-drift. (ch. xi)

Schematic criticism may try to fit such passages into the symbolism of the whole: they are transformation scenes, and the novel is concerned with the nature of bare truth; they are anticipations and analogies: Mrs Waddy hopes that the Arabian splendours will not vanish, and they do. Richmond Roy, like Ahmed, shoots his arrow, and loses the prize, but his desert is his own. Janet is a kind of Peribanou, sharing her role with Clara Goodwin. Richmond Roy describes himself as a magician, but his magic has limits. But the chief interest of such images is surely their local glow of excitement. They come mainly at the beginning of the novel, before the romantic excitement appropriate to the child remains improperly with the man. Meredith seizes a story from the Arabian nights (the arrow, the magic carpet and the apple are borrowed properties) and uses it impressionistically and rapturously, as he does the natural scene, changed by fog or fire or the child's eye.

Both the fixed implication and the resonance of image and symbol are often inevitably exaggerated by the critic's thematic diagram, whose serial nature tempts us to plot their course. Meredith does use symbolic scenes and accompanying images in a serial pattern which gives them some moral definiteness and lingering power, but this is by no means his only method. The trail is a confused one, blurring symbols, contradicting associations, often using powerful images for a temporary effect, pushing analogies before us but refusing to hold them steady. The trail is strewn with apparent analogues—Telemachus points unmistakably towards Harry's relation with Richmond Roy, but the analogy is crossed by the implications of Calypso and Penelope. Temple rejects the sinister Germanic forest's history and wants to call it Hades, but Harry, characteristically 'making the worst' of 'the dusky scenery of a strange land', tells the story of the beautiful girl betrothed to the earth-dwarf, in return for a sack of jewels. It is no use trying to apply this as an analogy to Harry and Ottilia, even though there is the resemblance of a pledge, a swerving, a high price, and the tempting echo in Ottilia's 'poor little gnomes' when she leaves Harry after they have found their love in the storm. The elements are there but wrongly composed. And later when the dark forest echoes in imagery it is displaced: 'she . . . plunged me headlong down impenetrable forests'—'she' is Julia Rippenger, not Ottilia, as a neat map-maker would expect. The applications of scene and inset story switch about like dislocated analogy. Sometimes the symbols are blurred or the echoes discordant in a recognition of genuine ambivalence. Meredith may treat an analogy as Donne sometimes does, turning it like a globe to see the implications of its other aspects and revalue it. This may extend a symbol or make— less 'organically'—a witty or sensuous assertion of the image in its own right. Sometimes the apparent symbol is there to contribute to mood and atmosphere, not to develop a moral theme. The pattern is sometimes morally logical, sometimes shifts kaleidoscopically and almost haphazardly. I would not claim that these impressionistic blurrings and dislocations are made in the interests of realism—though this may sometimes be the case—but merely suggest that Meredith's imagination often moves in this kind of broken pattern, and that the schematic critic, assuming as he usually does that the imagination aspires to complete 'organic' unity, will find intransigent material in this novel. The schematic mapping of patterns of imagery and symbolism must sometimes abrogate its neat formulae in order to recognize the place of casual and wayward richness like this.

CHAPTER V

Implication and Incompleteness:
George Eliot's *Middlemarch*

Harry Richmond is a rambling novel, concentrated in its moral subject and point of view, expansive in action, symbolism and imagery. *Middlemarch* provides us with a model for the expansive form, in its large scope, multiple variations, and freedom from the restrictions of either aesthetic or ideological form. Many of its structural features—antithesis and parallelism, anticipation and echo, scenic condensation—are those we also find in Meredith and indeed in Henry James, but in a restricted range. Not only is the organization of *Middlemarch* much less conspicuous and indeed less elegantly symmetrical than that of a novel by James, but there is never any sacrifice of truthfulness to the achievement of aesthetic ends. The form is the means to the ends of good story, moral argument, and the imitation of life. It is much more naturally plotted than the ideological novels, less dependent on coincidence and less restricted to crisis, and it shapes its moral argument tentatively through character and action, instead of shaping character and action in accordance with dogma. There are no strong climaxes like those at the end of *The Ambassadors* and *Jane Eyre* which complete a pattern or clinch an argument but distort the appearances of life.

The act of comparison is a dangerous tool in criticism. We may too easily select the material for comparison in order to back our prejudices and preferences, and if we shift the comparison, and put *Middlemarch* beside *Le Rouge et le Noir*, or *Anna Karenina*, or *Lady Chatterley's Lover*, we must modify our sense of its expansiveness and truthfulness. *Middlemarch* is a large, free, and truthful novel (to keep fairly close to James's terms but to reverse his judgement) but it has its own special restrictions. If we compare it with the novels I have just mentioned, novels which resemble it in social and psychological material to a sufficient extent to make the comparison viable, then we should use the word 'realism' more warily in our praise of George Eliot.

Middlemarch is only restrictedly truthful in its treatment of sexuality. The consequence is not only to make us use the word 'realism' warily but also to look hard at our praise of its formal unity. For one of the interesting features of this restriction is that it is uneven. The novel does not reveal a consistent restriction but a lop-sided one.

This restriction is present in George Eliot's early novels, too. It is, for instance, possible to argue that although the sexual desires of Maggie and Stephen, in *The Mill on the Floss*, are frankly dramatized, in general conception and in tense detail, the sexual implications of Maggie's relationship with Philip Wakem would have been more moving and incisive if they had gone beyond hints and implications. The sexual *lacunae* in *Adam Bede* are even plainer. Hetty's seduction by Arthur is dramatized in minute psychological detail, through the point of view of both characters. Arthur's desires are presented largely by implication and in symbol, but such symbols as the violent ride away from temptation and the unthinking ride back towards it are sufficient to give them substance. I do not have in mind an absence of physical detail but an absence of relevant emotional statement when I suggest that this sexual embodiment of Arthur throws into high relief what remains unsubstantial in Hetty. Her brilliantly recorded fantasy-life is remarkably lacking in sexual detail, but nowhere does George Eliot draw our attention to this conspicuous absence, or comment on its causes and effects, as she does with all other dramatized aspects of Hetty's mind and feelings. She tells us that Hetty is hard, but not that she is cold. The lack of sexuality seems to be the product of omission rather than of reticence, and it will not do, I think, to excuse the omissions on the ground that they are conventional or historically necessary. Hetty and Arthur are not a shadowy idyllic couple, but are subjected to the persistent analysis of both irony and sympathy. And Arthur is by no means a hero without sexuality.

It would be difficult to complain that the staled passions and live humiliations of Mrs Transome lose anything by being portrayed in a Victorian novel, though we may notice that her 'past' is shown retrospectively, in the novel's past, which possibly removes some of the difficulties of sexual delineation. The important thing, as I have already stressed, is not the absence of sexual realism achieved through a detailed clinical report, but the absence or presence of that psychological realism which makes the characters appear as sexual beings. And in spite of conventions of reticence, I would claim that George Eliot writes about Maggie and Mrs Transome and Gwendolen, Arthur, Stephen and Grandcourt, as creatures of sexual vitality, desire, and commitment. It is because of their sexuality that they are vulnerable, moved, aggressive, or threatened: sex enters not only into the 'portraits' but into the causality of the action. The passions and conflicts of these characters are sufficiently vivid and particular to make her moral argument meaningful despite changes in sexual morality.

In the earlier novels she handles sexual situations which she is able to make fairly explicit. There is no doubt that Janet is driven to drink by a sadistic drunkard, no doubt that Hetty is seduced and becomes pregnant, no doubt that Mrs Transome has committed adultery, even though George Eliot does not always give names to the situations and relationships. Her refusal to give names is probably less a matter of social decorum than a matter of dramatic effect.

Our curiosity and tension, and our troubled identification with secrecy, privacy, or anxiety, is brought about by local evasiveness and lack of explicit naming. We do not know immediately what Mrs Transome has done, nor do we know immediately that Hetty is pregnant. Our lack of information is justified by their furtiveness or pride. Our mere suspicion matches their understandable retreat from the subject. In these instances George Eliot withholds information in order to create tension and shock or decorously follows the reticence and evasiveness implicit in the situation.

In *Middlemarch* George Eliot is dealing with a situation which she cannot even name, and her evasiveness and suggestiveness, her retreat and approach, deserves close attention. Her refusal to be explicit is so marked that many readers do not even notice that there is anything which she is refusing to be explicit about. She is reticent—not, I claim, silent—about the Casaubon marriage. This reticence, because it is not silence, is compatible with a truthful and complete account of what it was like for Dorothea to be married to Casaubon, and what it was like for Casaubon to be married to Dorothea. We may not see the point at once, but when we do, I suggest, everything fits. But the novel's truthfulness is not sustained. In Dorothea's relationship with Will we have much more than a refusal to name the passions. We have a refusal even to suggest them. She is reticent about Dorothea and Casaubon, but she leaves things out in her treatment of Dorothea and Will. The omission is both an unrealistic element in an unusually realistic novel and the cause of imbalance. We can make the criticism in terms of truth and in terms of form. *Middlemarch* has often been praised as a great realistic novel and, more latterly, as a triumph of unified organization, but both its realism and its unity are flawed.

This flaw has to be uncovered in some detail. There have been many commentaries on the novel, but its delineation of sexuality has been glanced at very shyly or neglected utterly.

Critics may have sometimes assumed that the sexual implications of the Casaubon marriage are obvious. It is true that they form only a part of the moral and psychological action and are easily subsumed in a general account of the great trials and smaller triumphs of Dorothea Brooke. I do not want to give the impression that the novel has been misunderstood because critics have not recognized the impotence of Casaubon. This is a part of the story, but not the whole. But I want to bring out this part, and for several reasons. Some readers interpret this reticence as omission, and their view is encouraged by a generalized notion about the absence of sex in Victorian fiction, and in turn encourages this notion to persist: only in a Victorian novel could we have such an asexual view of a marriage. Some readers think that the omission is there, but is unimportant: the question does not come up, the failure of the marriage has nothing to do with sex. Some even respond rather perversely to what clues and cues we are given, and see Casaubon as physically repulsive, like Hardy's Phillotson, or even sadistic, like Grandcourt in *Daniel Deronda*. These are some of the views I have met—though not in print. One published view is that of John Hagan, in an article in *Nineteenth Century Fiction*: '*Middlemarch*: Narrative Unity in the Story of Dorothea Brooke' (June, 1961). Mr Hagan calls Casaubon 'a sterile ascetic'. We can all agree as to his sterility, but I think George Eliot tells us something about its cause. Calling Casaubon 'ascetic', however, seems as appropriate as calling Sir Clifford Chatterley ascetic. Neither of them has to make any effort to subdue the flesh.

George Eliot never tells us that Casaubon is impotent. Like most English novelists of her time, she is reticent, sometimes evasive, about sex. *Middlemarch* appeared twenty years before *Jude the Obscure*, and if we compare it with contemporary novels in France and Russia, it leaves out a lot. Everybody knows that Dickens was interested in the social aspects of sex, but contrived to write at length about

a prostitute, in *Oliver Twist*, without giving her a local
habitation or a name which would be unpalatable in family
reading. Sex as an aspect of personal relations scarcely
comes into Dickens, but George Eliot is plainly giving her
action some sexual substance in *Adam Bede*, *The Mill on the
Floss*, and *Daniel Deronda*. Her domestic drama seems restrained when we compare her with Tolstoy, but restraint is
not the same thing as omission, and if we confuse the two
when discussing *Middlemarch* we are surely imprecise when
we proffer the favourite words of praise like 'adult' and
'realistic'. I am not claiming sexual realism for George
Eliot. D. H. Lawrence allows himself total explicitness and
is moreover interested in aspects of sexual behaviour which
do not concern *Middlemarch* in any way. George Eliot writes
within a restricted convention of reticence, and is emphasizing sensibility rather than sexuality. But if we look at the
sexual implications of Casaubon, and see what they contribute to the moral and social pattern of the novel, George
Eliot's dramatization of the conflict between life-values and
death-values—Eros and Thanatos—will appear to have a
good deal in common with *Lady Chatterley's Lover*. Certain
Iliads, as Carlyle reminds us in *Sartor Resartus*, acquire new
extrinsic significance over the years, and it is possible that
the twentieth-century reader of *Middlemarch* sees this correlation of sexual and social values with exaggerated clarity.
When we isolate a theme we invariably appear to exaggerate its prominence, but I hope I am isolating something
which is an important and neglected part of the novel.
Middlemarch uses the sexual theme not merely in order to
confront life more truthfully, but in a significant bracketing
of social criticism and individual moral affirmation. The
rescue into love, which is a theme in many novels besides
Middlemarch and *Lady Chatterley's Lover*, involves some
social diagnosis of personal failures in feeling and relationship. It makes a symbolic equation of social and sexual
energy in ways which hold both terms in equal tension. The

virile rescuer can be a vivid symbol of social revolution; the decadent society can be seen as a cause of individual sterility; the failure of love can be explored causally—in the condensed causality of symbolism—and generalized. Such symbolism is condensed: it is not necessarily true that reactionaries are sexually impotent, and in these novels their impotence functions as metaphor. But this is more than rhetoric. There is some literal truth in relating the capacity for loving individuals to the capacity for loving humanity, and although the sexually impotent may be capable of love, the novelist can use both kinds of impotence and energy as mutual reinforcements. Unfortunately, *Middlemarch* does not make this reinforcement in a sufficiently complete fashion. The rescue and its implications are blurred and softened by an inadequate rescuer. One of the many reasons for discussing the Casaubon marriage is the light it has to throw on the character and role of Will Ladislaw. But this is to anticipate. The first thing to look at is the Casaubon marriage itself.

It would be misleading to say that the first real crisis in Dorothea's development is the sexual failure of her marriage. George Eliot's main emphasis is emotional, not physical, and though this emphasis may be in part attributable to the reticent treatment of sex, it is mainly caused by George Eliot's chosen situation—the frustration and collapse of a general marital failure. Casaubon's impotence is part of a larger incapacity for life, an incapacity we also find in Sir Clifford Chatterley. There is, however, one important difference between the two characters. In both the novelist is using physical impotence—I suppose 'unrealistically'—as a sign of basic sterility. Sir Clifford's impotence, caused by a war-wound, is made the cause of his imaginative and emotional failure. Lawrence uneasily combines an account of psychological causality with a metaphor. George Eliot avoids this causal account. Casaubon's physical impotence is seen neither as cause or effect of his general impotence. It is one of many symptoms. And even if we recognize that its appearance in the cluster of other symptoms is metaphorical and not realistic—there are presumably intellectual egoistic failures, incapable of proper human relations, who are sexually potent—his impotence is a fine stroke, which does more than complete a total picture of failure. It brings out Dorothea's ignorance and ardour, and society's irresponsibility in 'smiling on propositions of marriage from a sickly man to a girl less than half his own age' (1st edition, 1871-2; dropped in later editions).

Unless we see the sexual implications of Dorothea's crisis in Rome, George Eliot must seem to be vainly expending much of her satire and her sympathy. The author's reticence finds dramatic reason (or excuse) in the character's reserve: 'No one would ever know what she thought of a wedding journey to Rome.' But by the time we reach this enigmatic comment on Dorothea's reticence we have heard many frankly explicit doubts and fears about her marriage. Such doubts are voiced by several characters, though never to Dorothea. Each point of view is isolated and tempered by the prejudice of the speaker into a local effect of vagueness or ambiguity. Such ambiguity disappears as the impressions converge.

Let us look at some of these separate but converging points of view, noticing that they appear in several ways. There is the author's analysis of Dorothea's consciousness, ironically neighboured by an analysis of Casaubon's which is deliberately non-committal on first appearance. There is the spirited commentary of some biassed and unreliable spectators.

Dorothea has been frequently analysed and I will therefore merely pick out one or two relevant features. She is healthy, ardent, idealistic, young enough to be Casaubon's daughter, and very innocent. Her innocence is brought out strongly in her misunderstanding of the motives and affections of Sir James Chettam and in the explicit contrast between her and her sister, the more knowing and 'worldly-wise' Celia. It is Dorothea, not Casaubon, who tries to be an ascetic. She tries to renounce and rationalize her response to the glow of jewels and the joys of riding. Like Maggie, she knows too little about her own instincts to be able to adopt the ascetic role with safety. She has theoretical ideals of marriage ominously expressed in references to fathers and teachers, Milton and Hooker. She creates an image of her own nature and an image of ideal marriage which matches Casaubon's with fatal perfection. She defends his 'great soul' against Celia's distaste for his looks and habits. There is, of course, the additional irony that even measured by this theoretical ideal of marriage, Casaubon falls short: he is not a Hooker or a Milton in intellect or scholarship, and his soul is a little one, if we can fall into George Eliot's way of measuring souls. But this irony is not immediately relevant to my argument, and I mention it only to stress the selective analysis I am making. If Dorothea were right about her own emotional needs—which she is not—she would still be in for intellectual and moral disillusion. It is the emotional and physical shock which I want to bring out here.

When we see her in Rome, through Naumann's shrewd perception, she is standing in her Quakerish garb beside the statue of Ariadne, then thought to be the Cleopatra. George Eliot deliberately reminds us of both Ariadne and Cleopatra, and the association with Ariadne, forsaken after all her efforts in her maze, is as relevant as the sensual association with Cleopatra which gives extra point to Naumann's comment on the 'fine bit of antithesis'. The girl and the statue are not as different as all that, despite appearances.

Next we see her weeping, feeling a tendency to 'fits of anger and repulsion', disturbed by the violence and incoherence of Rome and by Casaubon's deficiencies of sensibility and explanation. Both she and Casaubon are irritable and nervous, and when she begs him to let her help in his work, 'in a most unaccountable, darkly-feminine manner . . . with a slight sob and eyes full of tears', she explains that she 'can be of no other use'. She asks if he is 'thoroughly satisfied with our stay—I mean, with the result as far as your studies are concerned'. Before Ladislaw's scepticism has made her doubt the value of Casaubon's research she has already begun to feel doubts about the future years 'in her own home', realizing that 'the way in which they might be filled with joyful devotedness was not so clear to her as it had been'. The main action of disillusionment is expressed in the response to Rome, which startles and bewilders her, while Casaubon comments 'in a measured official tone', quoting authoritative opinions on Raphael, for instance, with Cupid and Psyche picked out for special illustration. There is direct comment too, when George Eliot observes, with meticulous qualification, that this frustration and disappointment might have 'remained longer unfelt' if there had been ardour and tenderness:

> If he would have held her hands between his and listened . . . or if she could have fed her affection with those childlike caresses which are the bent of every sweet woman, who has begun showering kisses on the hard pate of her bald doll, creating a happy love within that woodenness from the wealth of her own love. That was Dorothea's bent. With all her yearning to know what was afar from her and to be widely benignant, she had ardour enough for what was near, to have kissed Mr. Casaubon's coat-sleeve, or to have caressed his shoe-latchet, if he would have made any other sign of acceptance than pronouncing her, with his unfailing propriety, to be of a most affectionate and truly feminine nature, indicating at the same time by politely reaching a chair for her that he regarded these manifestations as rather crude and startling. (ch. xx)

This describes a failure in feeling, and though there seem to be physical implications, it is certainly no clear indication of impotence. But this account is set in a context of highly critical comment which is frankly physical, and not primarily concerned with Casaubon's failures in tenderness or sensi-

bility. The initial physical contrast between Dorothea and
Casaubon is presented in descriptive detail: Dorothea's
health, her 'grand woman's frame' and—at a significant
point, just before Mr Brooke is to announce Casaubon's
proposal—'maternal hands', contrast with Casaubon's
poor physique, white moles with hairs, and so forth. The
inequality of the physical match is not left to the reader's
inferences. Almost everyone who comments on the marriage reacts in protest and disgust. The exceptions are the
over-tolerant and detached Cadwallader, and vague, self-
engrossed Mr Brooke, who feels that the complications of
women are equalled only 'by the revolutions of irregular
solids'. Brooke's own reasons for never marrying are
scarcely calculated to evoke respect and his hints about 'the
noose' and a husband's desire for mastery are carefully
placed in a very personal context. The fastidious Celia
shrinks, but we see her response in the context of her limited
egoism and superficial common sense. Sir James Chettam, as
the Cadwalladers point out, speaks with the partiality of a
young, handsome, and rejected suitor: 'Good God! It is
horrible! He is no better than a mummy', and 'What business has an old bachelor like that to marry? He has one foot
in the grave', and 'He must be fifty and I don't believe he
could ever have been more than the shadow of a man. Look
at his legs.' Later he calls him 'a parchment code' and claims
that 'he has got no good red blood in his body'. The out-
spoken Mrs Cadwallader, connoisseur of 'blood and breed-
ing', calls Casaubon 'A great bladder for dried peas to rattle
in'. She reassures Sir James that Celia will now be the better
match, since 'this marriage to Casaubon is as good as going
to a nunnery', and winds up her comment on his blood,
'Somebody put a drop under a magnifying glass, and it was
all semi-colons and parentheses'. Will's early hostility to
Dorothea makes him conclude that there 'could be no sort
of passion in a girl who would marry Mr Casaubon', but he
soon comes to rival the jealous eloquence of Sir James and

thinks of Casaubon as 'having got this adorable young creature to marry him, and then passing his honeymoon away from her, groping after his mouldy futilities'. He calls him 'a cursed white-blooded coxcomb' thinks of 'beautiful lips kissing holy skulls', and sees the marriage as 'the most horrible of virgin-sacrifices'. Will's reaction is the only one based on some comprehension of Dorothea's motives in marriage, and he uses the word 'fanatic' to cover both these and her rejections of art.

The implications of this chorus of disapproval go beyond a distaste for mere outward disparity of body and age. Incidentally, Casaubon is no obvious case of senile impotence,[1] and he may even be nearer forty-five than Sir James's suggested fifty. Mr Brooke tells Dorothea that 'He is over five-and-forty, you know'. Mrs Cadwallader is unambiguously thinking of sterility, from whatever cause, and although this aspect of the Casaubon marriage is dealt with reticently, it is an important thread in the pattern. It is much less prominent than it would be in the life of a heroine who had staked less on marriage as an education and a vocation, and it is true that nowhere does Dorothea long for children or lament their lack. But the subject is present everywhere except in Dorothea's actual words. It is alive, for instance, in the ironical contrast of her frustration with Celia's maternal complacency and Rosamond's miscarriage. It is alive, too, in imagery: there is the image of the elfin child withered in its birth, the strong image of the judgement of Solomon, in which Dorothea figures as the true mother and Rosamond as the false, and perhaps in this image used on one occasion for Casaubon's unresponsiveness to Dorothea: 'It is in these acts called trivialities that the seeds of joy are for ever wasted' (ch. xiii). Dorothea's lament is vague—it is for

---

[1] The actual age of characters who strike the modern reader as old is often surprising in earlier novels. Adam Verver, in *The Golden Bowl* (1905), is only 47 though he makes a more elderly impression and Charlotte says that he is responsible for the infertility of their marriage.

'objects who could be dear to her, and to whom she could be dear'. On one occasion she is thinking of Casaubon's will, which has provided for issue, but at no point in her innocent scheming for sharing the estate with Will, nor in Casaubon's reactions, nor in her discussion with Lydgate about having nothing to do with her money, does the obvious question of heirs come up. It is a marriage without ardour, without children, and, most significantly, without the expectation of children.

Casaubon does contemplate his possible heirs in drawing up his will, 'made at the time of their marriage' as we are told in Chapter xxxvii. It is now time to consider his expectations and reactions to marriage. George Eliot endows him with 'chilling rhetoric', both in love-letter and speech, but draws our attention to the possibility that this may not mean 'that there is no good work or fine feeling in him'. She also warns us of the unreliability of Casaubon's critics, forcing us to keep pace with the slow development of her action by her usual omniscient author's disclaimer of omniscience. But as soon as we enter the mind of Casaubon her irony and her pity confirm suspicion.

Casaubon, like many lovers, is looking forward to 'the happy termination of courtship', but for his own peculiar reasons—he will then be able to get on with his work. He has expected more from courtship. Relying, as later in Rome, on the appropriate authorities, he 'determined to abandon himself to the stream of feeling, and perhaps was surprised to find out what an exceedingly shallow rill it was'. Authority is discredited in the sad ridiculous conclusion, 'that the poets had much exaggerated the force of masculine passion'.[1] His own deficiency is the only uncanvassed explanation: 'It had once or twice crossed his mind that there was possibly some deficiency in Dorothea to account for the moderation of his abandonment; but he was unable to discern the deficiency, or to figure to himself a woman who would have

[1] The motto for this chapter (vii) is 'Piacer e popone, Vuol la sua stagione'.

pleased him better; so that there was clearly no reason to fall back upon but the exaggerations of human tradition'. Doubt continues:

> For in truth, as the day fixed for his marriage came nearer, Mr. Casaubon did not find his spirits rising ... though he had won a lovely girl he had not won delight. ... Poor Mr. Casaubon had imagined that his long studious bachelorhood had stored up for him a large compound interest of enjoyment, and that large drafts on his affections could not fail to be honoured. ... there was nothing external by which he could account for a certain blankness of sensibility which came over him just when his expectant gladness should have been most lively. ... (ch. x)

The imagery of low vitality covers his egocentric feeling for his wife and his work, his marital and his scholarly jealousies—a cloudy damp engenders all. George Eliot turns from such satirical comment to a straight unironical account of his conflict. He cannot tell Mr Brooke that he would like Ladislaw to leave Middlemarch because this would be a public admission of deficiency: 'To let anyone know that he was jealous would be to admit their (suspected) view of his disadvantages: to let them know that he did not find marriage particularly blissful would imply his conversion to their (probably) earlier disapproval ... on the most delicate of all personal subjects, the habit of proud suspicious reticence told doubly' (ch. xxxvii).

Although the self-regard is still the same, a new note has entered since his earlier assumptions that the failure in delight was attributable to poetic exaggeration. Even though Casaubon now has rather more grounds for blaming the failure on Dorothea, who has proved unexpectedly critical and independent, it is in fact hinted that he at least sees the possibility of other people thinking in terms of his 'disadvantages'.

This is the failure of ardour seen from his point of view. The question of issue is touched on only once in his internal commentary. This is in Chapter xxix, after their marriage, when George Eliot interrupts the expected sympathetic analysis of Dorothea to consider instead the 'intense consciousness' of Casaubon. Included in his marital balance-sheet are thoughts which go back to his previous expectations:

> On such a young lady he would make handsome settlements, and he would neglect no arrangements for her happiness: in return, he should receive family pleasures and leave behind him that copy of himself which seemed so urgently required of a man—to the sonneteers of the sixteenth century. Times had altered since them, and no sonneteer had insisted on Mr. Casaubon's leaving a copy of himself; moreover, he had not yet succeeded in issuing copies of his mythological key; but he had always intended to acquit himself by marriage. . . .

This account, moving backwards and forwards in time, is interesting in its ellipsis and juxtaposition. Casaubon's failure to leave a copy of his mythological key is ironically placed between the lack of any demand for him to leave another kind of copy and his (past) intention to acquit himself in marriage. It is a suggestive item, at least, and it is followed by an account of his lack of capacity for joy, which is in part a physiological explanation:

> To know intense joy without a strong bodily frame, one must have an enthusiastic soul. Mr. Casaubon had never had a strong bodily frame, and his soul was sensitive without being enthusiastic: it was too languid to thrill out of self-consciousness into passionate delight; it went on fluttering in the swampy ground where it was hatched. . . .

George Eliot insists on the lack of passion, claiming pity, not contempt, for such a 'small hungry shivering self', and ending with the mention of 'the new bliss' which 'was not blissful to him':

> And the deeper he went in domesticity the more did the sense of acquitting himself and acting with propriety predominate over any other satisfaction. Marriage, like religion and erudition, nay, like authorship itself, was fated to become an outward requirement, and

Edward Casaubon was bent on fulfilling unimpeachably all requirements.

Whatever ambiguity and evasion may at times come from
the convention of reticence, the double emphasis on emotional and physical deficiency, on the one hand, and sterility,
on the other, appear to converge in only one possible
explanation. It may be that the adult Victorian reader found
the suggestion more plainly pronounced than the modern
reader, having fewer cases of sexual frankness before him,
being more accustomed to implicit rather than explicit
sexual themes, and having no hardened prejudices about the
limitations of the Victorian novel.[1] Our expectations and
prejudices may well blind us to the implications of this
reticent mode of suggestion, but if we look carefully at these
implications I think we must say that Casaubon is sexually
very inadequate. We cannot definitely say that the marriage
is never consummated, but since Dorothea's nervous misery
begins in Rome, this seems highly probable.

As I said at the beginning of this chapter, I do not think
that the truthfulness of *Middlemarch* is impaired because
George Eliot does not tell us outright that Casaubon is
impotent. The very technique of implication has dramatic
advantages. Mrs Cadwallader might be expected to talk to
Sir James in knowing metaphor. Casaubon might be expected to avoid naming his deficiencies. Dorothea would only
weep in silence. On the other hand, I do not want to exaggerate this dramatic decorum. It could have been combined
with explicit naming, by the author or one of the characters,
and there is no doubt that social and literary restraint
governs the novel's reticence. There is no doubt, too, that
the sexual failure is only a part of Casaubon's generalized

[1] Since writing this I have seen David Daiches' little book on *Middlemarch* in
which he discusses Casaubon's impotence, making the comment that 'no doubt
the Victorian reader failed to see in the relationship between these two the matching
of impotence and sublimation' (*Studies in English Literature*, No. 11, p. 21). This
conclusion strikes me as very odd.

failure of mind and feeling. But the author does not distort the facts of nature and marriage: if we do not see the point, all is not lost, and the novel makes sense. If we do, then many of the small hints and details, as well as the larger tensions, make better sense, are more coherent and complete.

But where the novel shows the unhappy consequences of restricted treatment of sex is in Dorothea's relation with Will Ladislaw. Here is the psychological and structural flaw in *Middlemarch*. It is a psychological flaw because of a failure in truthfulness, a structural flaw because of the vivid presence of truthfulness elsewhere. I do not insist on describing the flaw in psychological and structural terms merely because of an interest in structure, but because I think the successes and failures which are combined in *Middlemarch* afford an interesting model for the formal critic. If we limit our definitions of form in fiction, as we so often do, to the organization of symbols, imagery, and ideas, then we may well pass over this failure. Recognition of this kind of failure forces us to review our ideas of form, especially our ideas of unity. It is possible to demonstrate the thematic and poetic unity of the novel: the themes cohere and persist throughout, and there is a mobile unity of imagery and symbol which has been analysed by several critics. But if we regard form in the largest sense, and think not merely of unity but of a more useful and less popular word, completeness, then we have to qualify our praise of the form of this novel.

The structural relationship of Casaubon and Ladislaw takes us back to James, and suggests that there is some point in his 'law' that the antithesis should be direct and complete. Up to a point the fable which lies at the heart of *Middlemarch* is clear enough. The three main characters are Casaubon, Dorothea, and Ladislaw. The fable may be called the rescue into love, and it has many forms in fiction. It is present in James's *The Bostonians*, in Gissing's neglected novel *The Emancipated*, in E. M. Forster's *A Room With a*

View and *Where Angels Fear to Tread*, in several of D. H. Lawrence's stories and novels, and in Meredith's *Lord Ormont and his Aminta* and perhaps in *The Egoist*. In all these novels the sexual rescue—from an old man, a woman, a sterile aesthete—has social implications. The rescuer is something of the Noble Savage and something of the Outsider, representing not only personal passion and fertility but the new blood needed and feared by the old establishment. Casaubon is, like Sir Clifford Chatterley, a cluster of different kinds of impotence. His futile mythological research, his nominal clerical function, his birth and property, all combine with his physical and emotional deficiencies to give him a significant place in the unreformed society. Like Sir Clifford, his assumption of Providential grace and favour for self and class gives him more than a merely personal deadness and egoism, though both in *Middlemarch* and *Lady Chatterley's Lover*, this is only an indirect generalization in a novel containing a great deal of overt political and social discussion. George Eliot's advantage over Lawrence, despite her sexual reticence, is that she creates an individual as well as a symbol, a man who feels the internal strain and loneliness of his position, a man torn by doubt and anxiety and pride, a man capable of stepping briefly outside this clearly marked moral category and on one occasion speaking to Dorothea with surprise and humility and recognition, capable of responding as a human being and certainly created out of sympathy and fellow-feeling. There is no possibility of an even identification with the characters in *Lady Chatterley's Lover* because they are not evenly animated, but Casaubon is presented as part of his environment, having a history, having the register of his differentiated consciousness, made of the same stuff as everyone else though warped, hardened, and self-regarding.

Ladislaw completes and answers these social implications. He is 'a kind of gypsy', defiantly declassé, grandson of a woman who rebelled against the Casaubon values of class and money, son of a woman who rebelled against the Bulstrode values of a Nonconformist respectable thieving line. His father is a musician, his mother an actress, and he is a dilettante and a Radical. As a Radical, of course, he also rejects the superficial and feeble liberalism of Brooke. Like Matey Weyburn in *Lord Ormont and his Aminta*, and Mellors in *Lady Chatterley*, he is a social misfit, a man seeking his vocation, and the poor man who wins the lady. But the mere absurdity of the comparison with Mellors or with Forster's Gino makes his deficiencies plain. As a Noble Savage he is a little fragile.

It may be objected that the very comparison itself is artificial, that I am complaining that Ladislaw fails to meet a standard set up by other novels and inappropriately applied to *Middlemarch*. Though I think the social implications of the love-story in *Middlemarch* are usefully brought out by this classification I am not judging Ladislaw by the general and external standards I may have implied, but by the expectations set up within the novel itself. Ladislaw and Casaubon make an excellent social antithesis in their roles, but an unequal sexual one.

The pattern is worked out very satisfactorily in terms of symbol and image. Dorothea is imprisoned in the stone prison of melancholy Lowick, in the labyrinth, in the dark tomb. Casaubon is the winter-worn husband, and the Minotaur. Ladislaw has a godlike brightness, is irradiated by images of light, is the natural daylight from which Dorothea is shut off. Images of darkness and light, aridity and water, enclosure and space, are strong. If Mellors turns up in the grounds of dismal Wragby in answer to Connie's question, 'What next?', Ladislaw is the unexpected 'someone quite young' found painting in the garden of Lowick. The generalized fertility symbols and more precise Persephone motifs are very subdued in *Middlemarch* when we compare it with *Lady Chatterley's Lover*, but they are present.

But poetic unity is not enough. The unity and antithetical

completeness of the imagery and symbolism of place and weather and appearances are not endorsed by the characters. Ladislaw is presented in terms of sensibility, not sensuality. The sexual implications of the imagery are substantiated in Casaubon—of course he can only refer to the opinions of *cognoscenti* when he shows Dorothea *Cupid and Psyche*—but not in the rescuing hero. At times, indeed, the imagery itself takes on and contributes to Ladislaw's idyllic colouring: there is a sexual implication when Casaubon concludes that the poets have overrated the force of masculine passion which is sadly lacking when we find Will 'verifying in his own experience that higher love-poetry which had charmed his fancy' (ch. xlvii). Those 'tall lilies' which he associates with Dorothea are more like a romantic detail from a Pre-Raphaelite painting, disturbing in their chastity, than like the shooting daffodils of *Lady Chatterley's Lover*. When the Cupid and Psyche symbol finds its antithetical completion, after Casaubon's death, the image is delicate and innocent, not strongly passionate:

She did not know then that it was Love who had come to her briefly, as in a dream before awaking, with the hues of morning on his wings—that it was Love to whom she was sobbing her farewell as his image was banished by the blameless rigour of irresistible day. (ch. lv)

The appropriate comment seems to be that at this point in the story she should have known. There are some Victorian novels in which it might seem captious not to accept such a lack of self-knowledge but *Middlemarch* is not one of them. George Eliot spends a fair amount of energy criticizing Dorothea's ignorance and short-sightedness but here remains romantically identified with this innocence.

Henry James is one of the few critics of Ladislaw to discuss his 'insubstantial character' in the appropriate terms. If his meaning is ambiguous when he complains in his review of *Middlemarch* (*Galaxy*, March 1873) 'He is really, after all, not the ideal foil to Mr Casaubon which her soul must have imperiously demanded, and if the author of the *Key to all Mythologies* sinned by lack of order, Ladislaw too has not the concentrated fervour essential in the man chosen by so nobly strenuous a heroine', it is clear that he is not merely thinking of Dorothea's soul when he later says more outspokenly, in the person of Constantius, 'If Dorothea had married anyone after her misadventure with Casaubon, she would have married a trooper' ('*Daniel Deronda*: A Conversation', *Atlantic Monthly*, December 1876).

I do not mean to suggest that our impression of Will is entirely romantic, innocent, and radiant. In his private thoughts about Dorothea's marriage, in his discussions with Naumann, in his excellently convincing relationship with Lydgate (especially where their masculine solidarity puts Rosamond's narrow femininity in its place), in his quarrels with Bulstrode and his differences with Brooke, he is detached, honest, and touchy. The relationship between Dorothea and Casaubon is presented in terms of sexuality, but that between Dorothea and Ladislaw is shown as denying it, and it is here that his masculinity falters. George Eliot is not hampered by the difficulties of describing actual love-making, though it is worth noticing that when Dorothea and Will touch each other they are at their most innocent and childlike. In the relationship between Maggie and Stephen, or the relationship between Lydgate and Rosamond, in this same novel, tension and desire are conveyed without physical detail.

In this novel sensibility acts as a surrogate for sensuality. This comes out in the presentation of Will as an artist, less marked by his ability than by impressionability. It comes out too in the sustained aesthetic debate which is the beginning of Dorothea's acquaintance with Will, and which has many implications. Dorothea is presented as a Puritan, and this makes for a special irony in her marriage—her self-abnegation has made the innocent blunder possible, but her ardour is there to suffer. It is Will who points out this

ignorance and sees the paradox, as Philip did for Maggie.
He preaches ardently on behalf of the art he loves, which
Dorothea distrusts, because of its obscure relation to the
hard realities, because of its apparently trivial delight in
beauty. Will's attempt to convert her to the aesthetic attitude
is most ironically placed in Rome, on her wedding-journey.
Will is presented as an aesthete of a special kind. His
impressionability is both praised and doubted: if it shows
itself in his response to art and in his restless trials as poet
and painter, it shows itself also in his sensitivity to other
people—to Lydgate, for instance, as well as to Casaubon
and Dorothea, where his understanding is less impartial.
But although he is carefully seen as a creature 'of uncertain
promise' (like Fred Vincy), he is given much more than an
effeminate aestheticism. His arguments in defence of beauty
are largely realistic attempts to persuade Dorothea into 'a
sturdy delight in things as they are'. Implicit in Dorothea's
first bewildered impressions of Rome is, I suggest, a reaction
to sensuality, though this is muted if we compare it with
Strether's response to the sensuality of Paris or the reactions
of Forster's heroines in his Italian novels. A neglected novel
which probably owes much to *Middlemarch* and which makes
a very explicit use of the landscape and art of Italy in the
education of the senses is George Gissing's *The Emancipated*
where Miriam, the Puritan heroine, is prepared for her
rescue into love by the sensual challenge of painting.
Miriam, like Dorothea, changes her views on art, but after
Mallard, the Bohemian hero, realizes that she is still alarmed
by sculpture, there comes an interestingly explicit dialogue
between Mallard and another male character in which this
is expressly accounted for by the mention of nudity. Mallard
rejects Philistinism in a brave picture of a domestic circle
where family reading will involve 'no skipping or muttering
or frank omissions' and where 'casts of noble statues . . .
shall stand freely about'. Journeys to Italy in the last century
presented special problems to Podsnaps and others.

Middlemarch was written twenty years before *The Emancipated*, but there are more than aesthetic implications in Dorothea's reaction to Rome:

Ruins and basilicas, palaces and colossi, set in the midst of a sordid present, where all that was living and warm-blooded seemed sunk in the deep degeneracy of a superstition divorced from reverence; the dimmer but yet eager Titanic life gazing and struggling on walls and ceilings; the long vistas of white forms whose marble eyes seemed to hold the monotonous light of an alien world: all this vast wreck of ambitious ideals, sensuous and spiritual, mixed confusedly with the signs of breathing forgetfulness and degradation, at first jarred with an electric shock, and then urged themselves on her with that ache belonging to a glut of confused ideas which check the flow of emotion. Forms both pale and glowing took possession of her young sense, and fixed themselves in her memory even when she was not thinking of them, preparing strange associations which remained through her after-years. (ch. xx)

The vague sensual implications here, and elsewhere, are related to her 'tumultous preoccupations with her personal lot', but not picked up in the ensuing debate with Will. This debate is indeed not continued throughout the novel, and lacks the clearer suggestions to be found in James or Gissing, who both correlate aestheticism with sensuality in their Bohemian characters. Will's Bohemianism[1] and his political activity are both related clearly enough, by opposition, to Casaubon's class-values, to Bulstrode's respectable Nonconformity, and to Brooke's brand of Radicalism, but they are less convincingly related to each other. If the idyllic and romantic innocence of Will's love for Dorothea is one weakness, his movement from art to politics is another aspect of his character which does not ring quite true. There is a slackening in the novel with the disappearance of the aesthetic debate which has carried so much of the antithetical play of social and sexual values. Will's political activity alone has a slighter reference, leaving his role as

[1] George Eliot's use of art to express social value owes much, I suspect, to *Culture and Anarchy*.

lover conspicuous and inadequate. We can see why the debate drops out. Once Dorothea sees her error in marriage, once she sees exactly where her fanaticism and self-ignorance have led her, the aesthetic debate is no longer required, and there are other ways of showing her aversion to her marriage. Her problem ceases to be one of bewilderment and becomes one of clear vision. Once she sees her marriage for what it is—which takes some time—her problem is chiefly that of accepting it, and living with it in activity and not mere resentment and despair. Dorothea cannot find Connie's solution, and has to live with her sterile marriage until her author provides the solution with Casaubon's death. Death often has to provide a substitute for divorce in Victorian fiction.

The weakness of the novel, and the weakness of Will Ladislaw, are located in his relationship with Dorothea. It is when they are together, physically or in thoughts of each other, that the romantic glow seems false and the childlike innocence implausible and inappropriate. In Will's other relations George Eliot can scarcely be accused of romantic softness, or of glossing over sexual problems. She keeps her heroine clear of any emotional conflict in her feeling for her husband and her feeling for Ladislaw, and here the moral scheme strikes the modern reader as being worked out at the expense of truthfulness. But although Will is shown as romantically rejoicing in the purity of Dorothea and in the impossibility of his love—'What others might have called the futility of his passion, made an additional delight for his imagination' (ch. xlvii)—this is only a part of the analysis of Will's emotions. In his relations with Rosamond the 'romantic' glow is strikingly absent.

His rejection of Rosamond is violent, shocked and fearful, and he deals a hard blow to her strong sexual vanity when he tells her that he loves Dorothea: 'I never had a *preference* for her, any more than I have a preference for breathing. No other woman exists by the side of her'. His declaration is a fine example of George Eliot's psychological truthfulness at its best, and it is neither exclusive nor obsessed, as declarations of love tend to be in many Victorian novels. George Eliot shows us the present, in William James's words, as more like a saddle-back than a razor-edge, for Will's confident rejection and words of love and loyalty are darkened by the shadow of the possible future. He looks over the edge of the present, though with pain and not with desire. Feeling, moral commitment, and time, are truthfully confused:

> When Lydgate spoke with desperate resignation of going to settle in London, and said with a faint smile, 'We shall have you again, old fellow', Will felt inexpressibly mournful, and said nothing. Rosamond had that morning entreated him to urge this step on Lydgate; and it seemed to him as if he were beholding in a magic panorama a future where he himself was sliding into that pleasureless yielding to the small solicitations of circumstance, which is a commoner history of perdition than any single momentous bargain.
>
> We are on a perilous margin when we begin to look passively at our future selves, and see our own figures led with dull consent into insipid misdoing and shabby achievement. (ch. lxxix)

Those critics who find Will Ladislaw a weak romantic conception, the under-distanced product of the author's fantasy, might reflect on the fact that few Victorian heroes are shown as contemplating adultery, and so coolly and miserably, in the moment of passionate commitment to the pure heroine. George Eliot is restricted in her handling of the central relationship in this story, but her treatment of the relations of Will and Rosamond, like her treatment of the Casaubon marriage, shows not merely her ability to admit realities commonly left out of the novels of her time, but to recognize uncomfortable truths often evaded or denied outside literature.

Middlemarch is full of such uncomfortable admissions. There is Mary Garth's moment of fantasy about Farebrother, when she glimpses possibilities of a relationship which might have advantages which marriage with Fred, whom she loves, will lack. There is the extreme irritability of Dorothea, punctuated by her impulse to love, but not removed by it. There is the hard truth which Caroline learns in *Where Angels Fear to Tread*, 'that wicked people are capable of love', shown with much less explicitness and fuss in the extreme case of Bulstrode. This kind of acceptance of the mixture of things is not confined to the hard truth. There is the comforting truth that we recognize with Lydgate, that even in the moment of passion, 'some of us, with quick alternate vision, see beyond our infatuations, and even while we rave on the heights, behold the wide plain where our persistent self pauses and awaits us' (ch. xv). If Will is capable of tolerating his vision of adultery with Rosamond, there is another shift of mobile moral category when Rosamond for one brief moment responds to Dorothea, or when Casaubon recognizes Dorothea's gesture of patient love. The recognition of human complexity blurs the clearly established moral categories, if temporarily, and can work in the interest of moral optimism and pessimism. George Eliot's choice of the tentative word 'meliorism' is clearly illustrated in her sense of the close neighbourhood, in human nature, of possibilities of the good and the bad.

Middlemarch, like most novels, has its formal simplifications and omissions which are determined by social and personal factors, but its expansiveness allows for many moments of surprising truth. We cannot say that there is a strict organization of category, of parallels and antitheses, which breaks down in the free admission of change and complexity. In describing the form of the novel we have to confront not a neat symmetry and clear unity which has additional details which seem to be added on, like grace-notes (if we admire them) or as wasteful and arbitrary strokes (if we do not approve), but a highly complex and mobile pattern. But this does not mean that we are left with no standards with which to judge formal success, and in at least one respect, as I have tried to show, it is necessary to criticize *Middlemarch* for a lack of balance and completeness. The demand for unity and the demand for truth should be inseparable. The inadequacy of the word 'unity' is suggested in this attempt to analyse form and truth as inseparable constituents of the good novel, for it would be true to say that *Middlemarch* would be a satisfactory unity if the asexual presentation of Dorothea's relation with Will were matched by a similar omission in the presentation of her relation with Casaubon. Completeness seems to be a better word than unity, including as it does the formal concept of equality of strengths with the concept of truthfulness. Who would exchange the flawed *Middlemarch* with its omissions made conspicuous by its suggestive reticence, for a novel where truth were reduced and mere aesthetic balance retained?

CHAPTER VI

Truthfulness and Schematism:
D. H. Lawrence

THE novel is seen in its freer forms in the work of D. H. Lawrence. Like Henry James, Lawrence is in some danger of passing an act of uniformity against novelists, but his aims and purposes are almost the exact opposite of James's. In James we find aesthetic values at their purest and most extreme; in Lawrence we find the violent rejection of any external artistic values of form and a passionate defence of particular truths. James rejects the loose, the accidental, and the arbitrary. Lawrence rejects the fixed, the deliberated, the conventional. Both of them use literary criticism for similar purposes of explaining and publicizing the individual values they prize as novelists, and in the process of idiosyncratic interpretation and judgement often do less than justice to other writers.

Even prejudiced vision has its insights, either of antipathy or sympathy. Lawrence's remarkable essay on Thomas Hardy, for instance, may read at times too much like an account of Lawrentian novels which happen to be about characters called Jude and Sue and Tess, but his essay on Galsworthy confronts us with a devastatingly shrewd analysis of imaginative sterility. Lawrence on Joyce, on the other hand, tells us more about the critic than the victim. His dislike of Joyce seems perfectly intelligible, even if we do not happen to agree with F. R. Leavis that one cannot admire both novelists. We might well argue that the formal deliberations and intricacies of *Ulysses* entail no loss of humanity, but there seems little doubt that they are strikingly unlike anything we find in Lawrence. Lawrence is at the very opposite pole from the 'impersonal' artist creating in silence and cunning, the God paring his nails at a distance from his creation. Lawrence's novels are as close to life as fiction can be, and when he pares his nails the bits get into the novel. 'Art', he writes in a letter to Carlo Linati, January 1925, 'art, especially novels, are not little theatres where the reader sits aloft and watches—like a god with a twenty-lira ticket—and sighs, commiserates, condones and smiles' (*The Collected Letters of D. H. Lawrence*, ed. Harry T. Moore, p. 827). In Joyce he found only the absence of life; I believe that he was wrong about this, but his scathing comments form a good introduction to the formal qualities of his own writing. He says, for instance:

> James Joyce bores me stiff—too terribly would-be and done-on-purpose, utterly without spontaneity or real life.   (*The Collected Letters of D. H. Lawrence*, p. 1087)

He dislikes not merely the artistic deliberateness of Joyce but what he sees, mistakenly I think, as the moral implications of psychological self-consciousness:

> It is self-consciousness picked into such fine bits that the bits are most of them invisible, and you have to go by smell. Through thousands and thousands of pages Mr Joyce and Miss Richardson tear themselves to pieces, strip their smallest emotions to the finest threads, till you feel you are sewed inside a wool mattress that is slowly being shaken up, and you are turning to wool along with the rest of the woolliness. . . .

> And there's the serious novel: senile-precocious. Absorbedly, childishly concerned with *what I am.* 'I am this, I am that, I am the other. My reactions are such, and such, and such. And, oh, Lord, if I liked to watch myself closely enough, if I liked to analyse my feelings minutely, as I unbutton my gloves, instead of saying crudely I unbuttoned them, then I could go on to a million pages instead of a thousand. In fact, the more I come to think of it, it is gross, it is

uncivilised bluntly to say: I unbuttoned my gloves. After all, the absorbing adventure of it! Which button did I begin with?' etc.

The people in the serious novels are so absorbedly concerned with themselves and what they feel and don't feel, and how they react to every mortal button; and their audience as frenziedly absorbed in the application of the author's discoveries to their own reactions: 'That's me! . . .' (op. cit., p. 518)

In the minute particulars of *Ulysses* Lawrence found no larger or warmer morality, and his gross parodies of the stream of consciousness are chiefly interesting because they reveal his hatred of moral triviality. He attacked the introspective narrative because he saw it as merely egocentric analysis which ignored really urgent social questions:

Supposing a bomb were put under the whole scheme of things, what would we be after? What feelings do we want to carry through into the next epoch? What feelings will carry us through? What is the underlying impulse in us that will provide the motive power for a new state of things, when this democratic-industrial-lovey-dovey-darling-take-me-to-mamma state of things is bust?

What next? That's what interests me. 'What now?' is no fun any more. (op. cit., p. 520)

If James has the highest possible artistic respect for the novel, Lawrence has the highest possible human respect. The crude violence of his contempt brings out the consistency in all his arguments. If he dislikes the trivial question, he also dislikes the conspicuous artistry, the exaggerated experiment which brings such rational deliberation into art that life and feeling seem to be destroyed. For the kind of novel which shows, or seems to show, as much interest in form as *end* as in form as *means*, he has no time at all. It is not surprising that he made Sir Clifford Chatterley's impotence show itself not only in industrial research and mechanized relationships but in the 'deadly' art of an analytical novelist.

His dislike of rational deliberation and egocentric analysis comes also from his desire to keep faith with the principle of change. 'The old stable ego' of Victorian fiction and the analysis of Joyce both seemed to Lawrence static forms imposed on the fluidity of human nature:

All things flow and change, and even change is not absolute. The whole is a strange assembly of apparently incongruous parts, slipping past one another.

Me, man alive, I am a very curious assembly of incongruous parts. My yea! of today is oddly different from my yea! of yesterday. My tears of tomorrow will have nothing to do with my tears of a year ago. . . .

In all this change, I maintain a certain integrity. But woe betide me if I try to put my finger on it. If I say of myself, I am this, I am that!—then, if I stick to it, I turn myself into a stupid fixed thing like a lamp-post. I shall never know wherein lies my integrity, my individuality, my me. I *can* never know it. It is useless to talk about my ego. That only means that I have made up an *idea* of myself, and that I am trying to cut myself out to pattern. Which is no good. You can cut your cloth to fit your coat, but you can't clip bits off your living body, to trim it down to your idea. (op. cit., pp. 536-7)

His dislike of a static pattern is closely connected with his distrust of ideological schemes. Here we come to one important difference between Lawrence and earlier novelists. Not only the frankly dogmatic novelists like Defoe and Hardy, but also the freer novelists, like George Eliot and Meredith, have imposed moral categories on their characters and action. Although it is undoubtedly true that Lawrence had a less simple and rigid moral classification than George Eliot, the important difference for us shows itself in the relatively static pattern of the Victorian novel and Lawrence's attempts to break this down. I would not claim that he always succeeded in breaking it, and he himself makes the claim only for novels written after *Sons and Lovers*.

The comments I have quoted come indeed more than ten years after *Sons and Lovers*, which is, at a superficial glance, a novel written in a conventional form. It uses both the conventional model of a categorical organization of character, and of a developmental form. But if we compare even this early novel with the traditional use of categories and development, some differences will emerge. In the novels of George Eliot, in spite of the unselective flow of sympathy, and in spite of the acknowledgement that the same humanity can inform widely different moral categories, there is a basic division into sheep and goats. We can say, with some definiteness, that characters are selfless or selfish, that they are, in E. M. Forster's terms, capable of love or not. There are many occasions when categories break down. Rosamond's response to Dorothea shows the author's recognition of a common moral potentiality in all her characters. Rosamond is a fine example of an egoist imprisoned within her own desires and fantasies, yet even Rosamond can on occasion make contact with another human being on terms alien to her desires and fantasies. But the contact is temporary, heralding no final conversion, and the selfish desire returns to insulate and injure. Bulstrode's relationship with his wife and his subtly self-beguiling belief in himself both indicate a similar refusal to make characters entirely stereotyped, but there is no doubt that the moral category is plain and plainly labelled. In Dickens such moral categories are usually even more plainly fixed. There is no doubt about our placing of Mrs Jellyby or Chadband or Esther, in *Bleak House*. There is not only a rigid form of moral category but even a difference in mode, so that we feel no possibility that Pecksniff, in some ways morally similar to Bulstrode, should be shown as morally self-conscious, no possibility that Rosa Dartle, should, like Rosamond, act even momentarily 'out of character'. *Sons and Lovers* presents us with interesting examples of categorical form blurred by truthfulness.

Its use of the conventional form of *Bildungsroman* is also interesting. What I have already said about the sheep and goats categories in Victorian novelists like Dickens and George Eliot has, of course, to be modified. The segregation of characters into moral categories appears in novels where part of the interest—and a very important part—depends on the movement of some characters from one category into another. Both in Dickens and George Eliot—and in Jane Austen before them—the novel hinges on a central moral conversion. This is frequently seen as the process of growing up. *Emma*, *Great Expectations*, and *The Mill on the Floss* are novels where the hero or heroine comes of age, grows out of the innocence, illusions, expectations, egoism, and all the not-so-fatal flaws of youth. But the process is emphatically moral rather than psychological, and the pattern is generally speaking an optimistic one, qualified though it may be, in the novels of Dickens and especially those of George Eliot, by patterns of deterioration. In *Sons and Lovers* the pattern is one of psychological growth, with, I suggest, little moral implication. We are concerned with Paul's development, but Lawrence emphasizes the growth away from the family, in particular Paul's struggle to free himself from his mother, and there is no implication that Paul is becoming 'a better man' as there is with the maturing of Emma or Pip or Maggie.

The pattern of development cannot be separated from the pattern of categories. Paul's development is created by his relations with his parents and his mistresses, and these in turn are determined by the relation between Mr and Mrs Morel. Here, it must be noticed, moral distinctions are drawn, but in a curious and interesting way.

Morel is defined and judged in moral terms. He is the ignoble savage whose ghost, it seems to me, is not finally laid until his passion, his class, and his skill, are used in the Noble Savage Mellors,[1] in *Lady Chatterley's Lover*, after sporadic attempts in *The White Peacock*, *The Lost Girl*, and many of the tales. In *Sons and Lovers* the relationship between the rough and passionate man and the gentle sensitive woman is shown as wounding, not as healing. Morel is

---

[1] The verbal relationship of the names is interesting: 'Mellors' contains 'Morel'.

presented as guilty, and in some places is castigated as surely
and significantly as Dickens castigates the cruel or apa-
thetic mothers who appear in most of his novels. We see him
as brutal, dirty, slovenly, and capable of using his brutality
and slovenliness in order to humiliate his family—a subtle
piece of social observation. Lawrence can say explicitly that
he has 'denied the God in him'. But most readers of the
novel will have reacted immediately to my comparison with
Dickens. Morel is not created wholly out of this judgement.
He is very much more than a study in deterioration, very
much more than a humiliating and guilty contrast to the rest
of the family in their difficult social and cultural climb.
Lawrence wrote to Rachel Annand Taylor in 1910, 'I had
only one parent' and is said to have expressed the wish (in
1922) that he had given his father a fairer showing in *Sons
and Lovers*. The interesting fact remains that *Sons and Lovers*
is not written out of the feeling that he had only one parent,
but that it gives Lawrence's father a fair showing. Morel is
not created out of antagonism alone. Lawrence blamed his
father, and made Paul blame his, and he dramatizes brilliantly
the son's shame and antagonism. But he also dramatizes
the vitality of the father, and humanity surely overrides both
judgement and aggression. The portrait of Morel is built up
from sympathy as well as antipathy. In his essay, *Morality
and the Novel* (op. cit., p. 529), Lawrence insists that the
novelist should not 'put his thumb in the pan', and though
he is speaking in a different context, we may use his own
words and claim that the power and truthfulness of this
novel shows itself in a refusal to put his thumb in the pan and
make of the portrait of his father an aggressive or negative
denial of individuality and life.

This contradiction in *Sons and Lovers*, which I would
praise for its truth, has been described and most strongly
criticized by Mark Schorer. In his essay, 'Technique and
Discovery' (*Forms of Modern Fiction*, ed. William Van
O'Connor, p. 19), he speaks of 'a psychological tension which

disrupts the form of the novel and obscures its meaning',
and says: 'Lawrence is merely repeating his emotions, and
he avoids an austerer technical scrutiny of his material
because it would compel him to master them. He would not
let the artist be stronger than the man.'

There is no doubt that there is a psychological tension in
the novel, and if our canons of form are the traditional ones
of clarity and conclusiveness—canons which do not fit even
the Victorian novel very happily—then I suppose we may
say that the tension disrupts this kind of form. But this is to
measure the actual form against a model, not to recognize
the nature of this novel's form as individual and appropriate.
If we demand a clear and consistent 'meaning' then the
second accusation makes sense, too, but the meaning of this
novel appears to me to reside in the tension. It is true that
there is a double point of view. We find that Mrs Morel is
praised and loved, Morel denigrated and hated, but shown
as overflowing the response of denigration and hatred.
Schorer would not accept this account of contradiction, for
he suggests that Mrs Morel is not presented with sympathy,
and this I find hard to see. Her self-righteousness and possessiveness indeed come through clearly, but so do her energy,
her sufferings, her sensibility, her courage, and her love.
There is tenderness both in described and dramatized feeling. Schorer suggests that Lawrence loves his mother but
also hates her for 'compelling his love', but this I think he
does not fully substantiate. If artists can be stronger than
men, *Sons and Lovers* might indeed be used as evidence.
Lawrence's own comments on his father show less sympathy
than the novelist's portrait of Morel.

The novel would have been less vulnerable to this kind of
formal criticism if Lawrence had possessed less insight, if
the book had indeed expressed the cry 'I had only one
parent'. Would Schorer prefer a novel which tidily backed
up the castigation of Morel (certainly present) with an
appropriate stereotype, or a novel which showed a totally

sympathetic mother-figure? His attack on the book seems to rest on the assumption that truth is single and simple, that the mother's love was merely crippling, that Morel is a passive victim. Lawrence's contradictions seem to me to incorporate a very likely ambivalence towards his parents and his loves.

For instance, Schorer accepts Jessie Chambers's account of Lawrence's distortion of the 'facts' as if she were in an unbiassed position. Unlike Jessie Chambers, Lawrence certainly offers more than one reason for Paul's failure with Miriam, suggesting that the crippling effects of his mother's love was one obstacle, Miriam's own ability to love 'only his spirit' the other. While I would not suggest that this is a literal and true account of Lawrence's relation with Jessie, there seems to be no reason for preferring her natural selection of the first obstacle. There are possible reasons for Schorer's preference of her account in the appeal of the classical schematism of an Oedipal pattern and the classical schematism of unity and simplicity. Both seem to be at the back of Schorer's key comment: 'The point of view is never adequately objectified and sustained to tell us which is true.'

Truth had no simple or single face for Lawrence. He may be caught in the mesh of his own predicament but he is not only writing out of his loves and hates, feeling and remembering the antagonisms and guilts of his childhood, but also remembering the qualities of real people. He saw the dangerous mother-love as a source of energy as well as a source of weakness. We might here merge Philoctetes with Oedipus and find a complex recognition of acceptance and blame, wound and energy, which may even have matched the facts. Lawrence's comments on *Sons and Lovers* show his very real awareness of some of the effects of his mother's love, but certain passages read like a defiance of Freud:

Paul loved to sleep with his mother. Sleep is still most perfect, in spite of hygienists, when it is shared with a beloved. The warmth, the security and peace of soul, the utter comfort from the touch of the other, knits the sleep, so that it takes the body and soul completely in its healing. Paul lay against her, and slept, and got better; whilst she, always a bad sleeper, fell later into a profound sleep that seemed to give her faith. (ch. iv)

Lawrence is conscious enough of the reactions of hygienists but he is presumably recollecting the physical tenderness of childhood. What would Schorer have him do with this kind of defiant loving memory? He could omit it or distort it in the interests of therapeutic explanation and formal clarity, but instead he leaves it to stand as a truthful affirmation of a common aspect of childhood love and need.

Lawrence himself, in the account of *Sons and Lovers* written to Edward Garnett on 14 November 1912, one day after posting off the manuscript to Duckworth, is quite aware of the so-called contradictions in Paul's love for Miriam. He says that Paul cannot love because his mother 'is the strongest power' in his life, and describes how Miriam, his first love, fights his mother for his soul, while his second love, Clara, gives him the 'passion' he has 'decided to go in for . . . leaving his soul in his mother's hands'. This seems to be a case where we can trust both the artist and the tale, even though Mark Schorer, following Jessie Chambers, sees a contradiction here. Paul's weakness is not 'disguised', as Schorer suggests, by Miriam's insistence on spiritual love. Whatever the distortions introduced by Lawrence in the portrait of Miriam (I am not claiming that he was likely to be more objective than Jessie, merely that she may not have been more objective than he was), the nature and source of the weakness, and the part played by the mother, is surely clinched by the second failure with Clara, which reveals the man's inability as the common element and the weakness. Lawrence is not offering a psychiatrist's diagnosis, but an account of human relations where the conflicts and causality are exceedingly mixed and complex, and if he wished to make Miriam the scapegoat, as Schorer suggests, he should have omitted Clara, or presented her very differently. In one sense, indeed, Miriam's failure in passion *underlines* Mrs Morel's failure with her husband's 'purely sensuous' nature.

In Lawrence's account of the story he says that the sons react to their father in hate and jealousy, and the reason for this is placed squarely on the responsibility of society and circumstances, which have put the mother in a position where she needs and uses her sons. He makes an important recognition here which Schorer does not mention. He attributes the sons' vitality to the passion felt by Mrs Morel for her husband, and while this may be an unscientific myth it is an appropriate comment on a novel which presents Morel both as a likely candidate for hate and jealousy and as a man for whom a wife had felt passion. Schorer comments that Paul Morel 'loves his mother, but he also hates her for compelling his love; and he hates his father with the true Freudian jealousy, but he also loves him because his wholeness has been destroyed by the mother's domination, just as his, Lawrence-Morel's has been'. This is described as a 'contradiction in style' and a 'confusion in point of view'. Let us look at two places where this contradiction and confusion might be said to appear.

Just before the passage in defence of sleeping with a beloved, comes a brief account of Morel who is trying to comfort and help but is irritating the child by hanging about awkwardly and undecidedly:

On retiring to bed, the father would come into the sickroom. He was always very gentle if anyone were ill. But he disturbed the atmosphere for the boy.

'Are ter asleep, my darlin'?' Morel asked softly.

'No: is my mother comin'?'

'She's just finishin' foldin' the clothes. Do you want anything?' Morel rarely 'thee'd' his son.

Here, I suggest, there is no confusion because there are two points of view. There is the author's voice and the child's, not a single ambivalent 'Lawrence-Morel'. The recognition of gentleness and the powerfully dramatized awkwardness and helplessness of the father stand outside the antagonism and rejection of the child's point of view.

On another occasion Lawrence uses his own words, not Paul's, to say that Morel 'had denied the God in him' and this is immediately preceded by a piece of wonderfully sympathetic dialogue which does much more than illustrate the reasons for this judgement:

Paul won a prize in a competition in a child's paper. Everybody was highly jubilant.

'Now you'd better tell your father when he comes in,' said Mrs Morel. 'You know how he carries on and says he's never told anything.'

'All right,' said Paul. But he would almost rather have forfeited the prize than have to tell his father.

'I've won a prize in a competition, dad,' he said. Morel turned round to him.

'Have you, my boy? What sort of a competition?'

'Oh, nothing—about famous women.'

'And how much is the prize, then, as you've got?'

'It's a book.'

'Oh, indeed!'

'About birds.'

'Hm-hm!'

And that was all. Conversation was impossible between the father and any other member of the family. He was an outsider. He had denied the God in him. (ch. lv)

This is certainly not done from Paul's point of view alone. While Lawrence is precisely and movingly conveying the clever child's embarrassment at bringing news to the father in his different world, he is also aware of the father's sad stilted gestures across the gulf.

This episode is followed by the vivid account of occasions when Morel is relaxed and energetic and part of the family. There is the story about the pit-pony, told in 'a warm way' so as to make 'one feel Taffy's cunning', and the pictures of

Morel at work, soldering metal, mending boots, or making fuses. In all this the Godhead of his vitality is present, he has confidence and energy, and he makes contact with his children. There is a juxtaposition of the good moments and the. bad, and what is impressive is the sympathy of imagination present even in the bad moments. This is helped by Lawrence's apparently vague time-scheme, which sometimes picks examples and anecdotes with the chronological arbitrariness of memory. It is not always clear whether one episode follows another in time or in memory. The overwhelming impression is of truthful report, both of antagonism and vitality. Paul's prayers for his father's death, and the 'happy evenings', have a kind of confusion which is true to the song of experience superimposed on the song of innocence. Lawrence remembers both his hatred and his father, and the character of Morel is larger and more sympathetic than a mere object of hatred, though it is probably impossible to determine how much of its vitality is due to truthful memory and how much to adult understanding. A tidier account which drew our attention to the two points of view might have said, for instance, 'It was not possible for Paul to feel pity'. But such formal discrimination does not seem necessary, and might even have removed the truthful effects of ambivalence. Lawrence was writing while his father was still alive, and although he had passed through the early love-affairs before his meeting with Frieda, the kind of clinical detachment advocated by Schorer might have been very difficult. Lawrence wrote this novel over a long period of time, so that both Jessie and Frieda were able to criticize and advise, and this may well account for one possible contradiction mentioned by Schorer. At the end of the novel Paul is freed from the temptation to follow his mother in what Lawrence described in the letter to Garnett as 'the drift towards death' and it is odd that Lawrence makes no suggestion, in this account, that the ending is explicitly and implicitly an affirmation:

But no, he would not give in. Turning sharply, he walked towards the city's gold phosphorescence. His fists were shut, his mouth set fast. He would not take that direction, to the darkness, to follow her. He walked towards the faintly humming, glowing town, quickly. (ch. xv)

Schorer suggests that this is not the expected conclusion to a novel about 'the crippling effects of a mother's love' but 'crippling' is his word, not Lawrence's. Although Lawrence does say that Paul is 'left naked of everything, with the drift towards death', he makes it clear that the mother's death is presented as a conscious product of knowing and wishing which will free Paul. This may be a crude version of the mother-love struggle, but Lawrence is writing from experience, not illustrating Freud, and whatever the actual results of his relationship with his mother may have been, by the time he came to finish this novel he had started what he believed to be a successful and mature relationship with a woman. Frieda does not come into the novel as the successor to Miriam and Clara, nor did she so rapidly succeed their prototypes in Lawrence's life, but Lawrence's affirmative energy at the end is written no doubt out of his feeling for Frieda. The discrepancy which Schorer notices is partly the result of the confused time-scheme, partly the apparent contradiction in the letter to Garnett. Yet this letter is true in one sense—Paul has nothing at the end but his refusal to follow the drift towards death. The burden of Schorer's complaint is that there is nothing in the novel to convince us that Paul could refuse to take this way to extinction.

I suggest that there are many things, that he never turns away negatively but always to fresh attempts. There is also the powerful social and imaginative urge for which his mother is responsible—she has urged her sons into life as well as held back their manhood. Lawrence solves the problem of the impediment by her death, which frees the energy which she has encouraged and made possible. This is both emotionally and socially very moving. The feeling of class—

its ambitions and insecurities—is something Schorer barely mentions but which cannot be left out of the causality of the novel or the growth of Paul.

This is a portrait of an artist who owed his mother both his wound and his bow. The confusions and contradictions which can be exposed in the novel if we compare it with simpler moral schemes, where there are plainer categories and more straightforward processes of development, are not the confusions of an artist utterly blind to the implications of his own situation. They are rather the transcribed confusions of life. Lawrence was in the habit of shedding his sicknesses in his writing, as Schorer notes, and his novels are often very self-consciously a running commentary on actual experience. The degree of invention in *Sons and Lovers* and *Women in Love* is very small compared with that in James or Meredith or George Eliot. I should not like to defend all Lawrence's structural untidinesses as the necessary explosions of truth: his handling of the first person narrator in *The White Peacock*, for instance, is a model of how not to do it. The narrator, Cyril, sometimes disappears from a scene without any explanation, sometimes overhears the most unlikely conversations, and is sometimes treated so vaguely or ambiguously that it is difficult or impossible to tell whether he is present, absent, or invisible. This is a gross case of technical incompetence, though no doubt springing from the problems of transcribing actual events. But the so-called contradictions in *Sons and Lovers* come out of a special kind of fidelity to individual truths. What was true does not remain true, what is recognized by the eye and mind is not always recognized by the heart. Lawrence superimposes several restricted and changing truths upon each other in a way which may well disturb conventional moral and narrative expectations. This novel may not give a faithful record of events and people, but it gives a faithful record of feeling.

In *Women in Love* we are a long way from the developmental structure which tenuously linked *Sons and Lovers* with earlier novels. Growth and change are much less clearly purposive, especially in Birkin, the central character, and the novel lacks the sequential unity and wholeness of the chronicle form. Its action is episodic and fitful, and only in its imagery and symbols can we find consistency and completeness. It has the antithetical form which we find in George Eliot and Henry James, but it is antithesis blurred or broken by human qualifications. At times it presents question and answer with the formal explicitness of debate and sermon, but its relationships are so particularized, and kept so close to the inconclusiveness of Lawrence's own experience, that the novel confronts us with questions unanswered, arguments given up in weariness, dogmatic prescriptions recognizably unworkable. Such hesitations are plainly present in the ending, however we interpret them,[1] but much of the movement of the novel is tentative and seems to refuse to abstract solutions from events. It is a book with a moral scheme, most certainly, but the scheme, as it is presented, is more like a hypothesis than a dogma. Lawrence is by no means indulgent towards his hypothesis and eventually admits his failure to provide actual proofs, combining doubt and hope and leaving Birkin to confront the intransigence of life. We may want to write 'disproven'[1] but the end of the novel, like the end of *Sons and Lovers*, is too close to experience for the artist to show himself as stronger than the man.

If James found *The Newcomes* and *War and Peace* loose and baggy, what words might he have found for *Women in Love*? Yet there are ways in which its concentration reminds us of James. It deals with a time of crisis in four intimately connected lives, and uses an intense pattern of symbols and imagery. It has, moreover, the special Jamesian concentration of a play of affinities. The absence of a conventional

[1] See W. W. Robson's excellent essay on the novel in *The Modern Age*, Pelican Guide to English Literature, for a different interpretation.

action and story-line throws the symbolic action and relationships into strong relief, and the symbolism is inseparable from the presentation of affinities. When Gudrun responds to Gerald's Nordic beauty this is not only sexual attraction but a psychic affinity which is developed in their relationship and in the symbolism. When Gudrun and Gerald, at a later stage in their relationship, react ambivalently to the ferocity of the rabbit, the incident gives us another image of their deadly affinity and their eventual death struggle. The familiar symbolic terms are accompanied by the less familiar unconscious affinity. Just as James uses his telepathic technique to achieve many short-cuts of exposition and action, so Lawrence, attempting to dramatize unconscious forces, often leaves out the expected naturalistic developments of event and human relationships. The relation between Birkin and Gerald, for instance, in its antagonism and its affinity, is not shown in naturalistic action. We do not have anything like the slow uncurling of events which explains the opposition of Caleb Garth and Bulstrode, or even of Lawrence's own Aaron and Lillie, in *Aaron's Rod*. Gerald and Birkin are largely presented in debate and discussion, with the history of their association left vague and undetailed, apart from the one striking example of the wrestle in the library. But the fight itself, like the debate, is presented in the medium of stated affinity of feeling. In the scene at the Café Royal where Gerald and Birkin both meet Minette, and Gerald is drawn to her while Birkin is repelled, there is a simple example of this use of affinity. Their responses have a place in the evaluative scheme of the novel, though they are much simpler than the responses of the two men to each other, or the reactions of Gerald and Gudrun. Lawrence shows the significant approach to and retreat from Minette as a sexual response with larger implications, and in the major relationships there is an even more complex response of the whole character—physical, emotional and moral. Lawrence is constantly aware of the sexuality of his characters, and this often means that he does not explain affinities and enmities, as earlier novelists explained them, but relies heavily on the rhetoric of sensation. It is not merely a matter of language, but also one of movement and rhythm. Lawrence may jump from mood to mood, or from intuition to intuition, giving no rational explanation or transition but keeping the sense of vagueness and mystery often stubbornly present in life. One difficulty lies in the erratic nature of such withdrawals: Lawrence puts in many highly explicit reflections and it is not easy to deduce a system from his vagueness and his definiteness.

Perhaps the most interesting affinity in the novel is that of Birkin and Gerald, which has been lengthily discussed by F. R. Leavis in his illuminating book *D. H. Lawrence: Novelist*. My excuse for going through much of the material of his study, much more briefly and crudely, is less my disagreement with him on some minor issues than the different context of my discussion. Gerald, like Sir Clifford Chatterley, is endowed with a cluster of symbolic attributes, which defines his representative role as deadly industrialist. This definition is expository rather than dramatic.

What may appear as vividly immediate is often a symbolic enactment, like Gerald's family relations, or his death. There are few ordinary dramatic actions of the kind which give *Sons and Lovers* its natural flow and density. It is difficult to dispute Leavis's comment that the novel 'contains a presentation of twentieth-century England—of modern civilization—so firsthand and searching in its comprehensiveness as to be beyond the powers of any other novelist . . .' but harder to accept his description of its 'wealth of vivid dramatic creation . . . the astonishing variety and force of the enacted life'. The portrait of civilization is largely conducted in the modes of debate and symbolic scene, and though debates and scenes are placed, both psychologically and morally, the expository insistence makes it, I suggest, misleading to praise it for 'dramatic creation' and 'enacted life' without distinguishing this enactment from that of many of Lawrence's other novels and stories. Most of Leavis's examples are, as he realizes, 'expository and historical' but he refers us to 'the half-dozen pages following the opening two of Chapter xxiv' in order to correct the impression he may have conveyed 'of a preponderant reliance on more distant modes'. It is true that these pages which give us the Crich family at the time of Gerald's father's death are immediate and concrete in dialogue and detail, but the impression of Gerald's annihilation and dependence evoked here relies heavily on the primary modes of debate and symbol which have established his identity and problems in the preceding twenty-three chapters. There are very few dramatic illustrations of Gerald's relationships with his employees, for instance, and those which do exist, like the conversation about the old man Letherington, dismissed by Gerald, or the brief detail about the widow's coals, merely draw our attention to the cursoriness of dramatic enactment. Lawrence dramatizes Gerald as a lover, but not Gerald in his managerial role, which gives his character his representative social sterility and is indeed necessary to define his dependence on Gudrun and the pressure of his will in their relationship. More typical of the presentation of Gerald is the chapter called 'The Industrial Magnate' which shows the explicit exposition which is 'remote' like the symbolic scene, but completely unJamesian, as in the following passages:

When Gerald grew up in the ways of the world, he shifted the position. He did not care about the equality. The whole Christian attitude of love and self-sacrifice was old hat. He knew that position and authority were the right thing in the world, and it was useless to cant about it. They were the right thing, for the simple reason that they were functionally necessary. They were not the be-all and the end-all. It was like being part of a machine. He himself happened to be a controlling, central part, the masses of men were the parts variously controlled. This was merely as it happened. As well get excited because a central hub drives a hundred outer wheels—or because the whole universe wheels round the sun. After all, it would be mere silliness to say that the moon and the earth and Saturn and Jupiter and Venus have just as much right to be the centre of the universe, each of them separately, as the sun. Such an assertion is made merely in the desire of chaos.

Without bothering to *think* to a conclusion, Gerald jumped to a conclusion. He abandoned the whole democratic-equality problem as a problem of silliness. What mattered was the great social productive machine. Let that work perfectly, let it produce a sufficiency of everything, let every man be given a rational portion, greater or less according to his functional degree or magnitude, and then, provision made, let the devil supervene, let every man look after his own amusements and appetites, so long as he interfered with nobody.

So Gerald set himself to work, to put the great industry in order. In his travels, and in his accompanying readings, he had come to the conclusion that the essential secret of life was harmony. He did not define to himself at all clearly what harmony was. The word pleased him, he felt he had come to his own conclusions. And he proceeded to put his philosophy into practice by forcing order into the established world, translating the mystic word harmony into the practical word organisation.

Immediately he *saw* the firm, he realised what he could do. He had a fight to fight with Matter, with the earth and the coal it enclosed. This was the sole idea, to turn upon the inanimate matter of the underground, and reduce it to his will. And for this fight with matter, one must have perfect instruments in perfect organisation, a mechanism so subtle and harmonious in its workings that it represents the single mind of man, and by its relentless repetition of given movement, will accomplish a purpose irresistibly, inhumanly. It was this inhuman principle in the mechanism he wanted to construct that inspired Gerald with an almost religious exaltation. He, the man, could interpose a perfect, changeless, godlike medium between himself and the Matter he had to subjugate. There were two opposites, his will and the resistant Matter of the earth. And between these he could establish the very expression of his will, the incarnation of his power, a great and perfect machine, a system, an activity of pure order, pure mechanical repetition, repetition ad infinitum, hence eternal and infinite. He found his eternal and his infinite in the pure machine-principle of perfect co-ordination into one pure, complex, infinitely repeated motion, like the spinning of a wheel; but a productive spinning, as the revolving of the universe may be called a productive spinning, a productive repetition through eternity, to infinity. And this is the God-motion, this productive repetition ad infinitum. And Gerald was the God of the machine, Deus ex Machina. And the whole productive will of man was the Godhead.

Even the family relationships are shown in the context of explicit diagnosis. Gerald killed his brother in their childhood, and this is clearly related to his unconscious impulse, defended as accidental by Gudrun, but argued by Ursula as murderous: 'I couldn't pull the trigger of the emptiest gun in the world, not if someone were looking down the barrel. One instinctively doesn't—one can't.' In the same way, Gerald's fears of aggression are explained by Birkin as the projection of his impulses.

Gerald's industrial role, his brand of Cain—related beyond him to his whole family and enacted in the present by the drowning of his sister, who kills her rescuer in death —and the Nordic symbolism which gives him his physical presence and his death amongst the snow, are all attempts to correlate deadliness with will and intellect. Gerald is freed from stereotype in several ways. First, he is made to feel the internal strain of his will and his use of human 'instrumentality', and Lawrence shows him feeling a terrible pressure which gradually cripples him. The will is not the whole of the man, but distorts him. Second, this residual character who feels the strain of what he represents is shown as a bewildered and uncertain human being. He is chiefly marked by certainty, especially as contrasted with Birkin, whom he calls uncertain, but he has his own uncertain moments too. If Lawrence came to hate Middleton Murry as a representative of hated values, he saw him as a person too, and the ambivalence may be reflected in Gerald, and in his relationship with Birkin. In their conversation both men are tentative, even though opposed, and Gerald's bewilderment is in part the impression left by many questions and vaguenesses. Although he is made to represent an intellectual and scientific deadliness, he is not clearly rational. 'He did not *think* to a conclusion', but 'jumped to a conclusion', we are told. When he is talking to Birkin, in the chapter called 'In the Train' he relies largely on feeling. His questions are not the Socratic questions which come from confidence, but doubtful and innocent, and his part in the conversation is full of vaguenesses. He takes time to re-adjust to Birkin's tirade, he looks baffled, he says 'I don't know', 'I never quite feel it that way', 'I don't know—that's what I want someone to tell me', 'I only feel what I feel', and 'I can't say'. In the chapter, 'Breadalby', the uncertainty is even plainer:

'I can't see what you will leave me at all, to be interested in,' came Gerald's voice from the lower room. 'Neither the Minettes, nor the mines,[1] nor anything else.'

'You be interested in what you can, Gerald. Only I'm not interested myself,' said Birkin.

'What am I to do at all, then?' came Gerald's voice.

'What you like. What am I to do myself?'

In the silence Birkin could feel Gerald musing this fact.

'I'm blest if I know,' came the good-humoured answer.

'You see,' said Birkin, 'part of you wants Minette, and nothing but Minette, part of you wants the mines, the business, and nothing but the business—and there you are—all in bits.'

'And part of me wants something else,' said Gerald, in a queer, quiet, real voice.

'What?' said Birkin, rather surprised.

'That's what I hoped you could tell me,' said Gerald.

It is not merely a matter of uncertainty, though this is important in a novel so much concerned with uncertainty. This dialogue is a typical part of the dramatized relationship between the two men. The queer, quiet, real voice of Gerald, like his straining towards and away from Birkin,

---

[1] It seems unlikely that this pun is accidental.

makes him very much more and less than a Nordic symbol, a Cain-figure, or an industrial magnate. If Lawrence's human detail is insistently thematic, his debates are given life and individuality. Gerald is also Gudrun's lover. His willed cruelty both attracts her and eventually repels her, but he is her victim as much as she is his. She is attracted by the savagery of the rabbit, and that episode brings them together in savage affinity. She is attracted by his willed brutality to the terrified horse at the level-crossing. When she comes to feel his willed and deadly impersonality making her an instrument too, she casts him off. But there is not merely a symbolic account of affinity and repulsion, but also her discovery of the appropriate replacement, in Loerke, her fellow-artist, another representation of brutality, imposed will, and mechanism. The symbolic pattern does not entirely act as a surrogate for ordinary action. Gudrun's exchange of Gerald for Loerke is understandable in terms of sexual aggression and attraction and in terms of the symbolic argument. Gerald's death in the snow is something to which Gudrun's rejection drives him, as well as being the final breaking of his self-imposed strain and the last enactment of the curse on the Crich family. Gerald is created out of hatred and out of love. If Gerald had been totally schematized, like Sir Clifford Chatterley, Birkin's own relation with him would have been impossible. The two men represent yet another shifting antithesis. They are opposed in values but linked by a mutual uncertainty which gives immediacy and conviction to their debates. They are linked also in need and love. Nor is their relationship consistent or progressive. Gerald rejects the *Blutbrüderschaft* but wrestles with Birkin and feels with him that this comes to the same thing. The ambivalence is not something we can only discuss in literary terms, it is an ambivalence which seems to come out of life.

This is also true of Birkin's relationship with Ursula. The vitality of this relationship has two aspects: intellectual contradiction and emotional variety. In Chapter V I gave as an instance of George Eliot's truthfulness her recognition that a man could be in love with one woman and yet envisage a possible commitment to another, brought about less by passion than by the mere drift of circumstance. If we put this besides Lawrence's truthfulness about human emotion, it looks elementary. One of his most important contributions to the realism of fiction, in theory and in practice, is his rejection of the kind of specialized emotion which is the basis of the Victorian novel and of many twentieth-century delineations of love. In the Victorian novel, you are either in love or not, it is an absolute state. What is more, love is shown as passionate, tender, protective, affectionate, loyal— the list might be indefinitely extended but the actual range would be limited. Lawrence demands a greater range:

> Love is a great emotion. But if you set out to write a novel, and you yourself are in the throes of the great predilection for love, love as the supreme, the only emotion worth living for, then you will write an immoral novel.
>
> Because *no* emotion is supreme, or exclusively worth living for. *All* emotions go to the achieving of a living relationship between a human being and the other human being or creature or thing he becomes purely related to. All emotions, including love and hate, and rage and tenderness, go to the adjusting of the oscillating, unestablished balance between two people who amount to anything. If the novelist puts his thumb in the pan, for love, tenderness, sweetness, peace, then he commits an immoral act: he *prevents* the possibility of a pure relationship, a pure relatedness, the only thing that matters: and he makes inevitable the horrible reaction, when he lets his thumb go, towards hate and brutality, cruelty and destruction. (*Phoenix*, p. 529)

In *Women in Love* Lawrence shows a multiplicity of emotion in the central relation between Birkin and Ursula. There is tenderness, loving intimacy, the more impersonal 'bestial' passion, and a constant struggle. I would not argue that Lawrence's personal and autobiographical material works entirely in the interests of realism, and in some ways this central relation is unrepresentative in a way in which the Victorian course of true love, for all its simplifications and omissions, is not. The detail of Lawrence's definition of sexual harmony appears to be alien to many of his readers. Birkin and Ursula are, moreover, free to reject the normal social implications of marriage, and reflect those special conditions which made it possible, indeed imperative, for Lawrence and Frieda to reject England and family ties. Their economic freedom is a rare thing, and their desires are to some extent personal rather than general—they are free to refuse to furnish a home in England, and free to make the symbolic choice and gesture of giving the beautiful chair to the unattractive and unloving couple who have no choice. One cannot claim that this is the kind of novel which explores the implications of love in a typical or extensive form, merely that it reflects Lawrence's own problems and attempts at solution.

If this reflection of private conditions makes the range narrow, within that range there is an honest attempt to show a sexual relation compounded of many emotions, and made up of antagonisms as well as harmony. This gives the ring of truth to the relationships, the characters, and the individual moments. The characters embody ideas only in the way in which real people embody ideas, in discussion, and in imperfect action. Birkin, in some ways a representation of Lawrence, is not shown as a converting hero, but as a man who grows uncertain as his ideas are transformed into action. Ursula's scepticism and intransigence, as F. R. Leavis insists, reflect Frieda's point of view. She argues against Birkin's views of sexual harmony, forces him to use the word 'love' which he is trying to deny, and puts her finger, both unfairly and fairly, on the weaknesses of his solution. We might put this in a literary way and say that Lawrence is truly dramatizing debate and individualizing his characters as well as presenting them as embodiments of value, but I think the more accurate way of reporting the novel's triumph is to say that its honesty is not a literary honesty but reflects an actual situation. Birkin gives up and gives in as one has to give up and give in. The compromises of love testify in the most pronounced way to the equality which he himself demands.

In the chapter called 'Mino', Lawrence adopts the symbolic device of showing his meaning in the relationship of the two cats, and Birkin makes the appropriate interpretation for Ursula:

'I agree that the Wille zur Macht is a base and petty thing. But with the Mino, it is the desire to bring this female cat into a pure stable equilibrium, a transcendent and abiding *rapport* with the single male. Whereas without him, as you see, she is a mere stray, a fluffy sporadic bit of chaos. It is a volonté de pouvoir, if you like, a will to ability, taking pouvoir as a verb.'

'Ah——! Sophistries! It's the old Adam.'

'Oh yes. Adam kept Eve in the indestructible paradise, when he kept her single with himself, like a star in its orbit.'

'Yes—Yes——' cried Ursula, pointing her finger at him.

'There you are—a star in its orbit! A satellite—a satellite of Mars —that's what she is to be! There-there-you've given yourself away! You want a satellite, Mars and his satellite! You've said it—you've said it—you've dished yourself!'

The argument which continues through this scene and others brings out the essential demand for equality in conjunction, lays bare the deficiencies of the symbols and metaphors which are tried and found wanting, suggests the dangers and implications of Birkin's certainty and also of Ursula's certainty, and ends with the capitulation in weariness: 'Let love be enough then. I love you then—I love you. I'm bored by the rest.'

This oscillation continues, with the significant punctuation of moments of separateness. There are times when Birkin, alone, hates and rejects women. There are times when Ursula, alone, makes the most violent and apposite

criticism of Lawrence's 'Salvator Mundi' touch, and lays
bare the basic flaw of the doctrine of equality which he
preaches in violence and at pistol-point. The novel contains
not only the important objections to its own argument, as
Leavis constantly insists, but also the practical demonstration of the equality of the lovers.

It contains too the demonstration of doubt. Birkin says
at one point that the important thing is the relation between
man and woman, but at other times this is consciously
contradicted by his acknowledgement of his need for Gerald.
Although this may at first sight also seem a reflection of a
personal and 'abnormal' need in Lawrence, it does, I think,
acknowledge the typical difficulties of love, love in a world
of other people, love which has to put out more than one set
of roots, love which may need more than one relationship. He
acknowledges too that love has its moments of 'bestiality',
and this is one of Lawrence's most controversial admissions.

Birkin's relation with Ursula, like Mellors' relation with
Lady Chatterley, is made up of many desires and gratifi-
cations. It is shown as mutual tenderness and normal sexual
harmony, but the doctrine of respected separateness also
allows a place for what Lawrence calls here 'the bestial', and
I think the place of bestiality is more clearly argued in
Women in Love than it is in *Lady Chatterley*. The language
which he adopts is not always successful. It is often extravagant, vague and inflated, even ludicrous. But it is easier
to criticize than to suggest alternatives, and Lawrence's
language for passion of all kinds exhibits the strain which
the commonly unspoken puts on the novelist's need to use
words. This is a characteristic passage, from the chapter
'Continental', where the banality of imagery in the first two
sentences and the chopped clumsiness and simplicity of the
rest suggest the difficulties and the range of solutions:

The flickering fires in his eyes concentrated as he looked into her
eyes. Then the lids drooped with a faint motion of satiric contempt.
And she gave way, he might do as he would. His licentiousness was

repulsively attractive. But he was self-responsible, she would see what it was.

They might do as they liked—this she realised as she went to sleep. How could anything that gave one satisfaction be excluded? What was degrading? Who cared? Degrading things were real, with a different reality. And he was so unabashed and unrestrained. Wasn't it rather horrible, a man who would be so soulful and spiritual, now to be so— she balked at her own thoughts and memories: then she added—so bestial? So bestial, they two!—so degraded! She winced. But after all, why not? She exulted as well. Why not be bestial, and go the whole round of experience? She exulted in it. She was bestial. How good it was to be really shameful! There would be no shameful thing she had not experienced. Yet she was unabashed, she was herself. Why not? She was free, when she knew everything, and no dark shameful things were denied her.

Lawrence here, as elsewhere, is arguing for the place of so-called 'perversion' in love, and whereas in *Lady Chatterley* he uses poetic language to convey the actual physical sensations, here he gives us the mixed feelings and recoil in Ursula's mind. The passage has considerable thematic importance since the 'degradation' here, celebrated with some ambivalence, seems to be related to the earlier and more obscure discussion of the African way of dissolution, associated with the image of mud, earlier than the 'phallic ways', and related by antithesis to the Nordic way of intellect. Birkin breaks off the long debate about the two ways of knowledge, in favour of another way, which he hopes to find with Ursula:

Suddenly his strange, strained attention gave way, he could not attend to these mysteries any more. There was another way, the way of freedom. There was the paradisal entry into pure, single being, the individual soul taking precedence over love and desire for union, stronger than any pangs of emotion, a lovely state of free proud singleness, which accepted the obligation of the permanent connection with others, and with the other, submits to the yoke and leash of love, even while it loves and yields. ('Moony')

Birkin has formally rejected the 'sensual subtle realities far beyond the scope of phallic investigation' but there may be, in this elliptical and difficult passage, the suggestion that in their night of 'bestiality' he and Ursula are using their freedom to enjoy the 'mud' which he has opposed to the ice. After the wild dancing at the hostel, he and Ursula are carefully contrasted with Gerald and Gudrun. There is accepted 'bestiality' in one room. There is icy willed impersonality in the other, where Gerald reaches the extreme of personal strain and acts most plainly in his function as 'a messenger, an omen of the universal dissolution into whiteness and snow'.

The antithesis is never a clear and simple one. As stated in 'Moony' it is given up utterly by Birkin in favour of the 'other way', but it comes back, I think, at the end, and the contrast between the two couples shows that the 'other way' has more in common with the river of dissolution and the mud—Birkin and Ursula are seen earlier as flowers of mud—than with the deadly cold of Gerald's mechanism and the final symbolic landscape where he meets his death. On the last page even Gerald's symbolic function disappears, and in the centre of the drama is the human relationship, vaguely formulated and unworkable, but still significant, between the two men as men. The triumph of Birkin and Ursula is not clearly opposed to the failure of Gudrun and Gerald, and symbolic schematism is replaced by the conversation of human voices, talking about the difficulties of human love. It is perhaps one of the most moving endings in Lawrence, and trails away in hope and doubt and questioning:

'Did you need Gerald?' she asked one evening.

'Yes,' he said.

'Aren't I enough for you?' she asked.

'No,' he said. 'You are enough for me, as far as a woman is concerned. You are all women to me. But I wanted a man friend, as eternal as you and I are eternal.'

'Why aren't I enough?' she said. 'You are enough for me. I don't want anybody else but you. Why isn't it the same with you?'

'Having you, I can live all my life without anybody else, any other sheer intimacy. But to make it complete, really happy, I wanted eternal union with a man too: another kind of love,' he said.

'I don't believe it,' she said. 'It's an obstinacy, a theory, a perversity.'

'Well——' he said.

'You can't have two kinds of love. Why should you!'

'It seems as if I can't,' he said. 'Yet I wanted it.'

'You can't have it, because it's false, impossible,' she said.

'I don't believe that,' he answered.

Those who might argue that *Women in Love* is a novel rooted in abnormality, trying to generalize very particular experience, will find some of their objections anticipated within the novel. If it is objected that Lawrence made impossible demands of human relationships, the novel will endorse the objections. Lawrence is doing something very rare in art. He is not achieving impersonality and psychical distance, not externalizing his ideas and experiences, but writing out of doubt and failure, expressing ideas in which he has only uncertain faith. This is the untidiness and uncertainty of incomplete and fumbling human experience, usually inappropriate material for art, which we expect to provide an ordered version even of disordered experience. It records a failed experiment, in living and in thinking, and it is as far removed as art can be from the blueprint which projects an ideal form on the mutability and incompleteness of experience. To deny its power is, I suggest, to have rigid canons of art and insufficient respect for the kind of honesty which can admit despair and doubt, not just in art, but in living too. Its powerful episodes are yoked together not in easy thematic supplement, or in smooth progress, but with the irregular rhythm and question-marks of life. If the actual problems seem alien to many of us, the course of the argument, in just this irregularity and questioning, is less alien.

In his last full-length novel, *Lady Chatterley's Lover*, the obvious autobiographical pressure seems less visible, and his human material cannot be so easily described as alien or unrepresentative. Connie and Mellors are in many ways the characters of fable. Their story is worked out in a much more ordinary and representative environment, and they are subjected to the common pressures of class, profession, and family. Unlike Birkin and Ursula, they are not free to cut the ties which bind them to England. They are very far from rejecting the biological and social consequences which link sexuality with family life. They are the last Lawrentian couple engaged in finding their destiny in the hard conditions of our Tragic Age, and they do not repeat the actual sterility of the marriage of Lawrence and Frieda.

Like *Middlemarch*, the novel is both a social and a sexual fable. It presents the Lawrentian doctrine of social hope in sexual love, but it gives the fullest play to the social causality which makes that ideal of sexual love doubtful and difficult to attain. When we compare it with *Middlemarch* we find immediately that the emphasis is placed on sexuality, on the sterile marriage of the Chatterleys and on the virility and tenderness of Mellors, the Outsider, Noble Savage, and Rescuer. Lawrence of course is aiming at a sexual frankness which may seem to make this comparison fanciful. If we take George Eliot as an example of a novelist who is forced into an oblique presentation of the sexuality inherent in her theme, and forced, for one reason or another, into softening the character of Ladislaw into a romantic shadow, at least in his relations with the heroine, we can take Lawrence as a remarkable example of a novelist trying to tell the whole uncomfortable truth.

There are many aspects of this truthfulness in *Lady Chatterley's Lover*, and I want to mention only a few of these. There is the admission of 'bestiality' even in a tender passion, based on a dignified mutual respect essential to sexual and emotional harmony. This has recently received some over-excited notoriety, no doubt partly because of the very different but equally inflammatory ways in which G. Wilson Knight and John Sparrow forced some readers to see what they had never seen before, and partly because Lawrence is telling an unpalatable truth about sexual relations. He is insisting on what Ursula calls the 'freedom' of the good relationship, a freedom to explore aspects of sensuality frequently hidden in fantasy, enjoyed in pornography, and often inhibited in so-called 'normal' sexual relations. Lawrence is here open to the charge of justifying personal perversions, but I think his insistence on the right to sexual variety should more properly be described as breaking down the walls which taboos and fears still put up, in life and literature, between the 'normal' and the 'abnormal', between unrestrained sexual fantasy and frequently restrained sexual practice, undescribed except in erotic or clinical contexts. This particular defence comes with a special shock in a novel which is in many ways a very romantic love-story, told with the aids of poetry and myth.

Lawrence is also uncomfortably truthful in his use of sexual language, which we are again familiar with in pornography but not in literature. I do not want to reiterate Lawrence's own violent defence of this language, but to suggest that he is making a linguistic experiment, not for novelty's sake, but in the interests of truth. Obscene language can be a language of love. Lawrence makes it clear that it is here the private language of his lovers, who, like other lovers, use it in intimacy and freedom, but who have a special need which makes it dramatically appropriate. Yeats spoke of it with a warm appreciation, as a forlorn poetry, 'ancient humble and terrible'. It is the language of isolation, and has a pastoral function within the fable. Connie is initiated into love and into its language, and we should observe in that language a significant correlation between the use of obscenity and the use of dialect. Mellors is the uneasy outsider, who speaks the language of the gentleman as well as the language of the gamekeeper, and there are occasions when he uses the tongue of his own class defensively or aggressively, to insist on the barriers which separate him from Lady Chatterley. When the barriers are down, he uses his first 'natural' words with tenderness and intimacy, and as a part of the initiation into love. He has to translate for Connie, and teach her the use of his language, and this is done with humour and feeling. We see her rejection of a dead rhetoric, which has lost the sense of relatedness with things, and her acceptance of free and vivid speech, which is, in the context of the novel, an essential part of her process of discovery and rescue.

Before we are allowed to hear the four-letter words, we are confronted with a dead poetic language, which is an evasion of relationships instead of an expression of them. The novel uses pastoral in a complex way, taking the intimate relationship with nature not merely as a fertility symbol but as a wider demonstration of activity. Sir Clifford's inability to form relationships is consistent not only with his physical impotence but with his function as scientist and mine-owner. He is the representative of an industrialism which has destroyed nature and used men as instruments of its will for profit. He is also a man of letters, and his attitude to nature is consistently literary, in the most sterile way. Connie gives him a glass of violets to smell, saying 'they'll revive again', and he answers with the quotation, 'Sweeter than the lids of Juno's eyes', which she rejects, saying, 'I don't see a bit of connection with the actual violets . . . The Elizabethans are rather upholstered'. The little episode is repeated two pages later, when Connie and Clifford are in the wood, and she picks wood-anemones to give to him:

'Thou still unravished bride of quietness,' he quoted. 'It seems to fit flowers so much better than Greek vases.'

'Ravished is such a horrid word!' she said. 'It's only people who ravish things.'

'Oh, I don't know . . . snails and things,' he said.

'Even snails only eat them, and bees don't ravish.' She was angry with him, turning everything into words. Violets were Juno's eyelids, and windflowers were unravished brides. How she hated words, always coming between her and life: they did the ravishing, if anything did: readymade words and phrases, sucking all the life-sap out of living things. (ch. viii)

The obscenities are the linguistic antithesis to this readymade literary language, which comes between her and life. The language which Mellors teaches her is also new to her, not readymade. Its rough naming of life is at the opposite pole from Sir Clifford's unresponsive use of literary language, its outrageousness functions like grim satire. The flowers she gives to Mellors are used in their love-making, and when Mellors observes 'Pretty as life' the natural equation is plainly made, and the antithesis completed. This part of the sexual ritual may strike us as ludicrous. Both the acts and the words of intimacy are indeed perilously exposed in literature, and may well fail in public communication, but they are here a consistent part of a truthful exposure and of a symbolic pattern. Mellors's respect for Connie's body and his respect for the earth are literally brought together, in opposition to Sir Clifford's general impotence.

The novel may perhaps show the difficulty of telling too much of the truth, though it is hard to separate its literary shock from its psychological shock. Its frankness in sexual content and language has very clearly a pastoral function, and the irony of Connie's rejection of the Elizabethan rhetoric is extended when we remember that the Shakespearean quotation from *The Winter's Tale* is itself taken from a conventional pastoral context. *Lady Chatterley's Lover* is pastoral with a difference, with the functions of Autolycus joined to the functions of Florizel, but the underlying pattern is still the same, with the seasonal contrast between winter and spring and summer correlated with the contrast between sterility and fertility. It was there, in a muted form, in the imagery of *Middlemarch*. *Lady Chatterley's Lover*, despite its attack on Elizabethan language, is in some ways very close to *The Winter's Tale*, which uses action as well as imagery to demonstrate the rhythm of the seasons and the rhythm of love. Lawrence is substituting coarse language for poetic imagery, and showing freedom and fertility in an extreme and naked dramatization. He is, however, not celebrating the rescue into love in an innocent and isolated way, and just as *Middlemarch* ends on a tentative note, refusing to idealize the triumphs of Dorothea, so the conclusion of *Lady Chatterley's Lover* gives full expression to the note of doom with which the novel began, 'Ours is essentially a tragic age, so we refuse to take it tragically'.

The book ends with Mellors refusing to look forward in unequivocal joy to their future, and to the birth of their child. He is acutely conscious of 'death and destruction' and of 'a bad time coming'. The seasonal rhythm is completed in his letter to Connie, marking the end of summer in its date, and extending to winter in its image of snow and praise of chastity. There are the tones of doubt mingled with love— 'If only one were sure'. Quintin Hogg, in the House of Lords debate on the novel, objected to its inconclusiveness, saying that if Lawrence were merely a novelist he might properly have left the novel unfinished, but that as a preacher he should have ended it conclusively. This is both to confuse and segregate the functions of novelist and prophet: Lawrence is a prophetic novelist, but he does not let the function of prophecy make an ideal and affirmative conclusion, nor indeed, judging from his letters, is he ever in the position, as prophet, to prophesy with certainty. The novel's darkness comes partly from his despair at the industrial Midlands, which he revisited just before he wrote it, but the combination of hope and doubt is a characteristic and truthful mixture which is as typical of his early writing as of his late.

There is one respect, perhaps, in which Lawrence's truthfulness fails him in *Lady Chatterley's Lover*. He says in *Morality and the Novel*:

The novel is the highest example of subtle inter-relatedness that man has discovered. Everything is true in its own time, place, circumstance, and untrue outside of its own place, time, circumstance. If you try to nail anything down, in the novel, either it kills the novel, or the novel gets up and walks away with the nail.

Morality in the novel is the trembling instability of the balance. When a novelist puts his thumb in the scale, to pull down the balance to his own predilection, that is immorality. (op. cit., p. 528)

I have already mentioned one of his examples of the novelist putting his thumb in the pan, the 'immoral' love story which shows love as the only emotion worth living for, and shows love as a highly specialized emotion. Lawrence shows the complexity of love, even in this novel where the structure of moral fable is clearer than in any of his other books. Mellors's reaction to Connie includes reserve, resentment, jealousy and doubt, and even their successful achievement of sexual harmony has room for casualness, a sense of the ridiculous, and, as we all know, the 'bestial'. If love is compounded of many things, so is hate, and I believe that Lawrence is guilty, according to his own standards, of creating too schematic a contrast between the object of Connie's love and the object of her hate. If George Eliot failed to complete the antithesis required in *Middlemarch*, Lawrence in his version of the fable made too neat an antithesis. Casaubon is a symbolic cluster, but seen from the inside, created out of compassion, and demanding sympathy. Gerald, in *Women in Love*, like Casaubon, fulfils certain functions by providing a stereotype of wrong values, but is also seen and felt as an individual, invaded by values, not personifying them. Sir Clifford, if compared with these two, is much more like a personification, and here I think the weakness of the novel lies.

He is not presented in an entirely unsympathetic way, for Lawrence speaks of the slow effect of his wound, and feels for him as a hurt man, a victim of war and society. But he rapidly becomes an assembly of symbolic parts, and—as with Gerald—Lawrence adds on the symbols in somewhat remote exposition, rather than showing them concretely, in dramatic detail. Sir Clifford is a psychological novelist of the kind Lawrence most abhorred, analysing trivialities in minute detail, worshipping the Bitch-Goddess of success, eventually finding another of her shrines in science. He becomes a representative not only of class and property but of aesthetic sterility and the technological revolution. In art and industry, Sir Clifford shows the same disregard for human relations, and his sexual impotence acts both as link and—rather oddly—as cause. Later, we see him reduced to horrid infantilism in his relation with the housekeeper, Mrs Bolton. Unlike Casaubon, he is not shown as growing less certain and confident as the action proceeds. Unlike Gerald, he does not feel the strain of his adopted values, does not cry out in bewildered questioning. We do not feel that he is influenced by his values but that he *is* his values. All his actions are marked by the same denigratory symbolic features: his theoretical and practical attitude to machines, to class, to 'his' trees, to Connie, to her possible child as 'his' heir, to sex, to culture, and to nature. There are one or two odd moments when he appears as a convincing human being, as when he is shyly embarrassed in conversations about sex, but these scenes themselves are shadowy debates rather than real actions. It is partly a lack of individuality, a failure which is often associated with an urgently ideological concept of character, though more often found in idealization than in denigration. Daniel Deronda is a good example. Sir Clifford seems to have been constructed according to an ideological blueprint. Lawrence says that he did not realize for some time that the paralysis was symbolic, and Frieda tells us that he felt the same identification with Sir Clifford as with other characters. But in spite of such external evidence—he is an implausibly motivated character. The failure is of more than merely local interest.

Lawrence was aware that in some ways Sir Clifford's

impotence presented a difficulty for the working out of sympathy. He says, in *Apropos of Lady Chatterley*, that 'it makes it so much more vulgar of her to leave him'. It is perhaps not so much a question of vulgarity as of omission. Connie's hate, which she comes to enjoy, can be pure and strong just because Sir Clifford is so unequivocally a composition of false values, and it is easier to hate values than to hate individuals. What the novel leaves out is just what *Middlemarch* puts in, the sense of the individual which makes the eternal triangle much more than a diagram of value. *Lady Chatterley's Lover* admits the social difficulty of the love of Mellors and Connie without much appreciation of any other difficulty. Sir Clifford's character is so constructed as to make it a virtue for Connie to leave him, and this appears to be a simplified departure from probability. Here Lawrence does seem to be putting his thumb in the pan. The result is a failure of omission, as well as several moments of sheer bad taste or implausibility. Mellors sneers contemptuously, to Sir Clifford's face, about his impotence. Admittedly, he is injured and goaded, but one would prefer the lover to be at least embarrassed by his rival's impotence. The fight is not a struggle between individuals but shadow-boxing. Mellors can hurl insults and Connie feel little conflict because Sir Clifford is conceptually rather than individually constructed and provokes or even demands reactions which would not arise in a comparable human situation. The total relationship is not constructed in this abstract fashion. Connie and Mellors, despite their strong typicality and symbolic status, have some human light and shade. Mellors, for instance, despite his burden of Lawrentian values, is individual and plausible and moving in his jealousy, his resentment, his fatigue, and at least some of his doubts.

I realize that this may sound like a literary discussion of something which goes far deeper than a literary problem of realism. Lawrence was capable of pure hatred and rejection —though it is necessary to observe that his violent rejection of the Murrys and Lady Ottiline Morell was followed by compromise and some measure of reconciliation. But his letters show that his personal hatreds, however caused, were often expressed in terms of pure values. Sir Clifford is probably not the product of an abstract ideological concept but of a genuine and powerful hatred for certain values. And there is the special difficulty that the actual content of Sir Clifford's values is deadness and sterility—a content it might well be hard to individualize. This is one of the reasons why it is interesting to put him beside Casaubon, a character similar in values but nevertheless endowed with individuality, and an internal presence, to both of which we respond with sympathy, and which make his moral implications all the more frightening. Sir Clifford, like Ladislaw, is the weak character in the social and sexual fable, but for very different reasons. Ladislaw's lack of sexuality makes him less plausible as an individual character and less effective as a carrier of meaning. Sir Clifford is a clear enough thematic character but lacks the particularity which animates the rest of the novel. He is an extreme instance of a novelist's failure to animate the resistant material of strong feeling and confident belief and inform the characters of fiction with particularity and truth.

Confronted with such schematism, in a novel which has moments of such particularized sensation, the reader is usually puzzled to read Lawrence's own comments on the symbolism and his own initial unawareness. He writes to D. V. Lederhandler, on 12 September 1919, 'Yes, the paralysis of Sir Clifford is symbolic—all art is *au fond* symbolic, conscious or unconscious. When I began *Lady C*, of course I did not know what I was doing—I did not deliberately work symbolically. But by the time the book was finished I realized what the unconscious symbolism was.' (*The Collected Letters of D. H. Lawrence*, p. 1194.) This comment is much more intelligible to readers of the earliest version, *The First Lady Chatterley*, a novel considerably less remarkable for its sexual realism than *Lady Chatter-ley's Lover* but very much freer from ideological imposition. Lawrence wrote this letter after finishing all three versions, and presumably his awareness of the symbolic implications of Sir Clifford began to harden into the schematic form which is visible in the characters of both Sir Clifford and Mellors. The first gamekeeper, Parkin, has none of Mellors's Lawrentian properties, of education, ambiguous class, and articulateness. If this difference makes his relation with Connie both less easy and less hopeful, it comes from a freer and more individual piece of characterization. But the really striking change is in Sir Clifford, who in the first version is not a psychological novelist, much less emphatically a scientific manager like Gerald, and much less egoistically representative of aristocratic possessiveness. There are traces of his scientific and managerial willed and deadly energy, and slighter traces of his establishment values, but there is nothing like the schematic cluster of symbols which make up the final version. Moreover, Sir Clifford is more humanely and sympathetically conceived in his relation with his wife. He means more to her, presents her with a more realistic *modus vivendi* as alternative to Parkin, does not initiate the suggestion that she should have a child by another man, and in his reactions to her suggestion is seen not as complacent, aristocratic, and inhuman, but as digni-fied, awkward, proud, feeling himself in no position to do anything but accept. Lawrence in the first novel is even rather vague about the importance of Sir Clifford's impo-tence, suggesting that it is an accident 'in character' with the man, though transforming his energies, but also suggesting that he and Connie came together out of a passion very different from anything suggested in the flashbacks at the beginning of the last version, which show their relation as sexually incomplete even before Sir Clifford's wounding. Lawrence may have begun by being unaware of the schem-atism of the novel but by the time he came to write the third version his awareness has just the worst effects, and it is interesting to observe that the naked realism and the deliberated generalization are both made more emphatic in the process of revision. It is sometimes assumed that Lawrence's method of total revision is more 'spontaneous' than the more common kind of piecemeal revision, but the history of *Lady Chatterley* gives little support to this view.

As in *Middlemarch*, the demand for truthfulness and the demand for satisfactory form go together. *Lady Chatterley's Lover* is weak where *Middlemarch* is strong, in the delineation of impotence, and the novel may be called structurally uneven, or incompletely truthful. Once again, the word 'completeness' proves more useful than the word 'unity', forcing us to look at the novel as fully as possible instead of reducing it to the scaffolding of symbols or imagery or the abstract diagram of its ideas. It is the whole matter which is informed by generalization, and this means that a failure to particularize may be a formal failure just as much as an intellectual inconsistency or a confusion of imagery. 'Just as much' is a careless phrase, but I let it stand in order to remind the reader that relatively few novels are thematically inconsistent, and that poetic confusion may be either functional as in *Harry Richmond*, or unimportant. It is true that many novels show a consistent pattern, in imagery, but there are also powerful local images which belong to no series, but illuminate the moment. What is essential is completeness of human particulars, which alone can satisfy us that the novelist is both able and willing to represent the human case in vividness and complexity. There are novels, like *Rasselas* or *Animal Farm*, which rely on the diagrammatic rendering of types rather than the complex rendering of particulars, and these are the novels which we describe as tracts or satires rather than novels. They stand at the opposite pole from Lawrence, and their consistency is won at the expense of human vitality. This is not to denigrate their form, merely to distinguish it from the form of the true novel.

They bring out too the aspect of Lawrence's form which I have been at pains to emphasize throughout this chapter—its tentativeness and freedom. The word completeness, which seems a good one to use when we want to analyse the forms of action and character, is inadequate when we come to the intellectual pattern. Lawrence's argument is often incomplete. But this is perhaps where all formal terminology breaks down. The incomplete story is here the truthful rendering of a genuine doubt or change. Robert Louis Stevenson and Henry James would exclude this intimate testimony to uncertain life from the art of fiction, but Lawrence's power and moving honesty seem more likely to challenge their criteria than to bow before their judgement. 'In a world so anxious for outside tidiness', Lawrence wrote to Linati, who had written an article on him, 'the critics will tidy me up, so I needn't bother', and 'whoever reads me will be in the thick of the scrimmage, and if he doesn't like it—if he wants a safe seat in the audience—let him read somebody else' (*The Collected Letters of D. H. Lawrence*, pp. 826–7). Lawrence's lack of conventional 'form' is intimately connected with his quality of life.

Author's Note 1971

Since the reprinting of this book does not permit any major recasting of the original text, I note here the fact which will be obvious to readers of recent English and American fiction, that my emphasis on Lawrence's openness of sexual discussion has become dated.

CHAPTER VII

Form and Freedom:
Tolstoy's *Anna Karenina*

TOLSTOY's treatment of a lifeless marriage and a passionate love stands at a great distance from both George Eliot and Lawrence. In *Anna Karenina* there is no rescue into love but a fatal uprooting which exchanges one form of sterility for another. The social and emotional picture is so different from that in *Middlemarch* and *Lady Chatterley's Lover* that there is no point in close comparison, but I should like to pick out one striking difference which is especially relevant to my discussion of structure and truthfulness. In their separate ways, both George Eliot and Lawrence failed to realize completely the three persons of their central triangle. There seems to be little doubt that the 'incarnation' of 'ideas' in *Middlemarch* is not wholly satisfying. In the case of Lawrence, in spite of an uncomfortably honest presentation of sexual vitality, the figure of Sir Clifford is diagrammatic rather than fully humane. These incompletenesses are not purely local: if one character or one relationship becomes schematic or distorted, then the novel suffers in many ways. I have expressed my own criticism in elaborate formal terms, but perhaps the simplest and also the most satisfactory critical response is the complaint that the novelist has not realized the complex human situation which he appears to be exploring. In Tolstoy's central triangle consisting of Anna, Karenin, and Vronsky, there is a fullness of incarnation both characteristic and rare. This rarity must be my excuse for considering here one novel I have not read in the language in which it was written.[1]

All the characters in *Anna Karenina* are equally vivid, equally complex, equally free from the simplifications of stereotype. In the character of Levin, who corresponds to the self-image we find in Dorothea and Birkin, there is a total absence of self-indulgence, partiality, or confusion. There is never any feeling that the picture is losing the sharpness of particular life and time and giving way to the diagram. There is never any sense that autobiographical pressure or fantasy brings with it a loss of distance, even though the novel is in many ways very close to the author's life. The autobiographical pressure might have been felt in the character of Levin and his wife, in details of the marriage, in the account of his early loose-living, his brother's death, and his conversion, but these episodes and characters have the same status and solidity as the invented material, like the story of Anna, which was based on fact but not on intimately known fact or persons. In the honest irresolution of the ending we find something very like Lawrence's appropriate form of doubting anti-climax, but the novel which is thus ended has a dense realistic texture of psychology and event, a large and surely handled social range, and a very sparing use of poetic and symbolic action. It is very different from anything Lawrence ever wrote.

At first sight it seems closer to *Middlemarch*. There is a similar multiplicity, clarified and organized by comparison, contrast, and repetition. There is a similar impression, local and general, of that imaginative respect for individuality which can defy the rigidity of moral categories, even though such categories are tentatively set up within the novel. There is a similar social and professional realism, though in Tolstoy the social and geographical range is greater, and the

[1] I have used the translation by Louise and Aylmer Maude. Readers interested in the deficiencies of Tolstoy translations should refer to R. F. Christian's *Tolstoy's 'War and Peace'*.

phenomenal world more vividly present. But if we restrict ourselves to these very broad structural comparisons we shall be trapped into concluding that the resemblances alone are striking. One of the disadvantages of formal analysis is its tendency to make individual forms come out of the schematic process looking very alike. It is useful to point to the structural resemblance between a concentrated novel and an expansive one since it enables us to demonstrate the art which shapes the large loose baggy monster. It is also useful to group the expansive novels together in order to isolate both their range and their composition. But it is also useful —and much more difficult—to try to define individual differences, since only in this way can we stay close to the unique quality of the work of art. At this stage in criticism, everyone will be prepared to defend the structure of the expansive novels, *en masse*, so it is important to attempt some discrimination. This is my chief reason for choosing to talk about a single novel in this final chapter.

One simple difference between this novel and *Middlemarch* seems to link Tolstoy with Lawrence. George Eliot does not always delineate sexuality even when the action seems to require it, whereas Tolstoy and Lawrence go beyond rendering sex in the obvious places. Tolstoy indeed gives us little actual sexual detail in *Anna Karenina*. He shows the relationship between Karenin and Anna a little more openly than George Eliot does in the case of Dorothea and Casaubon, but we do not see physical details of the relationships in *Anna Karenina*. There are some examples of frankness which were deliberately challenging, like the discussion of contraception, but it is not primarily for this kind of revealing open disclosure that we would praise Tolstoy's sexual realism. He does not separate the sexual vitality of people from their personality. It is not something switched on and off in certain special circumstances or with certain people. Both Tolstoy and Lawrence make the character's endowment include that sense of energy and life, both psychic and physical, which is hard to define though easy to spot. Vronsky, Oblonsky, and Levin are all strongly sexed men whose sexual vitality is communicated in their energy, whether this is displayed in eating, working, or riding a horse. It is not merely that Vronsky's horse-riding is a symbol of passion, Oblonsky's pleasure in food an indication of other fleshly indulgences, Levin's energy in the fields a hint of his sexual needs and difficult restraints. It is more precisely that Tolstoy does not separate a man's sexual energy from other forms of energy. His characters are significantly alive, self-delighting, sensuously and physically aware of themselves and each other.

Sexual awareness is also truthfully distinguished from sexual desire. Levin's uneasiness in the presence of Sviyazsky's sister-in-law is a delicately observed recognition of a tense sexual response without attraction. It is there, rather more purposively, in his recognition of the sexual element in Lydia Ivanovna's relations with Karenin. Some of these details, like Levin's response to the sister-in-law, form a massive impression of lifelike concreteness as well as giving the characters a rare continuity of feeling and sensation and personality. Some characters in novels are never shown in sexual vitality, others are shown as sexual creatures in some contexts. Tolstoy gives us a continuous impression of the whole person. In some respects this kind of detail is very important in the action. Lydia Ivanovna's feelings for Karenin determine his refusal to divorce Anna. Karenin's own lack of energy is also significant—he is not an impotent husband but has no sensuous delight or appreciative power. The latter endowment is one of the many details which make up our total impression of these characters' vitality, whether it is shown in the appreciation of food or the appreciation of sport or the appreciation of fine weather. The physical world is important for Vronsky and Oblonsky and Levin. Only the professional world of government evokes enjoyment from Karenin.

Tolstoy sees sexuality as part of the whole person, not as a specialized reaction of body and feeling in certain hallowed or interestingly unhallowed circumstances. This is also true of Lawrence, where the characters react to nature or animals or other people with the same energy and appreciation, coldness or artificiality, which marks their sexual relations. For Lawrence too personal vitality must include sexuality, and he disliked the romantic untruthfulness of specialized love-stories in which love is a single, simple, and exclusive feeling. He insisted that a relationship between a man and a woman included a whole range of emotions, and just as we see the sexuality of a man in his responses to many aspects of life, so we discover far more than passion and tenderness in his sexual relations. In Tolstoy as well as Lawrence we find in the sexual relationships the mixture and continuity of desire and antagonism, pride and tenderness, possessiveness and independence, *ennui* and energy, joy and disappointment. This complexity of 'love' is a part of his unified view of personality. No single emotion of pure love exists, no separation of sexual from non-sexual vitality. When Anna and Vronsky first make love, and we see them afterwards sharing shame and regret and the feeling of commitment, important aspects of their relationship are revealed without moral comment or sentimental distortion. On many occasions we also see them as blinded and absorbed, indifferent to the watching eyes.

When Vronsky loses the race and kills his mare the scene is not, I think, symbolic in the way suggested by Joyce Cary in his book *Art and Reality*. We do not have to translate the objects and events and see them as transparent windows for the main relationships of the action. They exist in themselves, as characteristic and particular demonstrations. Vronsky's fatigue and anxiety before the race link his love with his failure, in the most practical way. Here he is both energetic and miscalculating, as he is indeed in his relations with Anna, but the horse-race is a part of the whole continuous treatment of life—work, play, and love bring out the same energies and the same errors. Each moment has its convincing immediacy, and falls naturally into the total impression of character and action with the absolute minimum of artistic heightening. The mare does not stand for Anna, nor Vronsky's mistake for his 'failure' in love. Not only are the actual reasons and motives importantly distinct but the feeling for each of these losses is perfectly appropriate to the particular situation. Vronsky loses the race and kills the mare because his absorption in Anna leads him to miscalculate. He loses Anna and she kills herself for more complex reasons. And compare this scene (as Joyce Cary did, with odd conclusions, in my view) with the scene in *Woman in Love* where Gerald forces his horse to wait at the level-crossing. Everything in the scene is perfectly in character: the imposed will, the brutality, the worship of the machine. There is the significant impression made on Ursula and Gudrun, the generalization indicated within the action itself. All elements correspond perfectly with Gerald's relationship to his employees, to Gudrun, even to himself. If the Tolstoy scene is symbolic then it is so in a much more diffuse and imperfect manner. Gerald subdues the horse as he subdues other people. Vronsky is tired and tense and not in perfect physical control of his animal. In the one case there is exact allegorical correspondence, though the images and feelings are strongly rendered. In the other there is no exact correspondence but a consistency of feeling, though even this should not be too much exaggerated.

This is where the initial comparison with Lawrence breaks down. In Lawrence, despite his wholeness of character conception, the action often proceeds by a symbolic process. We may well perceive a relation between the man's treatment of the horse and his treatment of the woman, but in Lawrence—at least in this novel—the symbolic aspect is so prominent that it appears to determine the existence of the scene. In Tolstoy it is part of the natural flow of events, and symbolic only in the way in which events are symbolic in life, in their typicality which is only part of their nature and function. In Lawrence we see the wholly significant revulsion of Ursula and attraction of Gudrun: moral identity rather than human detail is what counts, and this is an understandable form of concentration in a novel of symbolic action. This is Lawrence's version of total relevance. Tolstoy's scene, on the other hand, has many facets and many functions. We see the simple human reactions of Karenin and Anna—her exposure and absorption, his observation and sense of decorum. But in each case the scene has to be related back to the novel. Even though Lawrence creates in Gerald a man who contains his humour, and cannot be equated with it, not a stereotype but a man driven and changed by self-stereotyping, in Vronsky Tolstoy creates a character who cannot be morally categorized without grave reduction of the richness of the novel. Gerald is created out of feeling as well as theory, and is an individualized character if we compare him with Mrs Wilcox or Sir Clifford, but he belongs to the accepted foreshortening of psychology in the symbolic novel. Tolstoy's scenes are relatively free because they act out the complex histories of truly complex characters.

When Lawrence's characters respond to nature—hurling stones at the moon's image, turning to the caress of earth after human assault, giving flowers in love—there is both crisis and symbol. Nature is made appropriately schematic. The moon's image is the destructive Hecate, the vegetation a primitive source of fertility and healing, the seasons in *Lady Chatterley's Lover* as dramatically adapted to the action as they are in *The Winter's Tale*. They are also sensuously realized, never mere *schema*. Human beings react to their natural environment in a morally purposive fashion: Birkin reacts to moon and earth in a process of causality in which he discards false relations and tries to define and discover the right ones; Connie's reactions to the countryside in spring show us her retreat from the sterile marriage, the aesthetic values, and the industrial devastation which ruins the natural scene and the natural man. In Tolstoy there is often this kind of significance in the natural world, as in the very first page of *Resurrection*, but nature is much more than a symbolic environment. The sense of natural activity and seasonal movement in *Anna Karenina* certainly underlines Levin's search, his fatigue and sorrow, his energy and love. But the natural world also exists most strongly in its own sensuous right, establishes new facets of character, and is an essential part of the novel's social documentation. Its climate, its vegetation, its animals, and its labourers confront the reader in primary vividness. Lawrence has harsh words for Tolstoy's old dead moral scheme, and for what he called 'a certain crudity and thick, uncivilised, insensitive stupidity' shared by Turgenev, Dostoievsky, and Tolstoy, but he speaks with admiration of his ability to set 'behind the small action of his protagonists the terrific action of unfathomed nature' (*Phoenix*, ed. E. D. McDonald, p. 419). 'Unfathomed nature' is a better phrase for Thomas Hardy than for Tolstoy but Lawrence is right to draw attention to this source of power.

Levin throws himself into the act of mowing with his labourers on the Mashkin Heights, but the account of the mowing is not a selected emotional symbol, showing his reaction to disappointment in love, it belongs naturally with his energy and sympathy and pride. He returns to his farm from Moscow, to find that 'spring had come, a glorious steady spring, without the expectations and disappointments spring usually brings'. Tolstoy gives us the vitality of spring, in the new grass, the sticky birch buds, the animals, and the rattle of machinery. He does exploit the natural implications in order to compare Levin's aspirations with the growth around him:

Spring is the time for making plans and resolutions, and Levin, like a tree which in the spring time does not yet know in which direction and in what manner its young shoots and twigs (still imprisoned in their buds) will develop, did not quite know what work on his beloved land he was going to take in hand, but he felt that his mind was full of the finest plans and resolutions. (Part II, ch. xiii)

The weather and activity of spring are made phenomenal to the character in many ways. Levin throws himself with special energy into his work and plans, because of the season. Moreover, the seasonal activity is negatively related to his feeling for Kitty: it makes external demands on his vitality, it gives him a sense of joy outside his grief and jealousy which keeps this in our minds—'On this lovely day he felt that the memory of her did not hurt him at all'. The physical phenomena of spring are large and vivid beyond the personal problem. The lovely weather makes him feel happy despite his feelings about Kitty. This in itself is an unusually honest psychological insight which takes us beyond the various kinds of pathetic fallacy which in George Eliot or James either make the character and the phenomena merge sympathetically as in the storm in *Middlemarch* when Dorothea and Ladislaw declare their love, or in the day of 'untimely June rain' when Maggie asks Fanny Assingham what she knows about Charlotte and Amerigo, or make the character's emotions isolated and distinct from the significantly unsympathetic weather as in Hetty's flight or Caterina's. The simple admission that a fine day can make us feel happy even if we have been disappointed or grieved is a part of Tolstoy's recognition of emotional complexity. This seems to involve him in showing the phenomena in their own vivid right, unmoved by the demands of story and emotion. The phenomena never become mere dramatic properties.

In Part II, Chapter xv, Levin and Oblonsky go shooting. We are made to feel both the sense of Kitty's presence, which for a long time they do not mention, and its unrelatedness to the pleasure and activity. After the splendid shooting Levin at last asks Oblonsky if Kitty is married. He feels 'so strong and calm that he thought the answer, whatever it might be, could not agitate him'. He is shocked by the news that Kitty is ill, and Tolstoy marks the personal absorption by telling us that Laska, the dog, looks at the sky and thinks that the interruption will make them miss the woodcock. They do not miss; they both shoot and Levin says exultantly that the bird 'belongs to both', then remembers that 'there was something unpleasant! . . . Yes, of course, Kitty is ill! But what can I do? I am very sorry . . .' and breaks off to praise Laska, 'Found? good dog!' and takes the warm bird from the dog's mouth. This is almost the opposite of James's presentation of phenomena in terms of obsession. The scene is free because Tolstoy is saying that men's griefs are complex, are not always wholly absorbing, that work or play can be exhilarating even at such a time. Because the phenomena are so vividly present—the creak of growing grass, the exhilaration of the hunt—the scene is free from symbol. The sharing of the bird might, in a novel by Stevenson or James, be made indicative of the common family interest, but even this rejected interpretation sounds ludicrous here.

Such vivid realism and complexity appear in different ways in the two following chapters, where Oblonsky makes the bad bargain with Ryabinin about the sale of the forest. Levin disapproves strongly, but he is feeling generally depressed and irritated—itself a sign of emotional flux, since his earlier reaction was to feel pleased that Kitty is sick and unhappy. Oblonsky realizes that Levin's jealous humiliation about Vronsky will colour all his reactions, 'knowing well that everything would now seem wrong to Levin', and observing that he is 'down in the dumps today'. But the Ryabinin affair has its own independent status, like the spring and the shoot, and Tolstoy makes it plain, although Levin's irritation is caused mainly by feeling insulted and therefore 'angry not with what had upset him but with everything that presented itself', that this is not an irrational feeling about a swindle. Ryabinin's face assumes 'a hawk-like, rapacious, and cruel expression', and Levin's anger is intimately related to his feeling for land and class and work. The two feelings merge eventually when Levin bursts out in fury at Oblonsky's comment that Vronsky is an aristocrat and therefore an attractive match:

> You talk of his being an aristocrat. But I should like to ask you what is Vronsky's or anyone else's aristocracy that I should be slighted because of it? . . . I consider myself and people like me aristo-crats. . . . You consider it mean for me to count the trees in my wood while you give Ryabinin thirty thousand roubles; but you will receive a Government grant and I don't know what other rewards, and I shan't, so I value what is mine by birth and labour. (ch. xvii)

The fury drives him into the admission that he has pro-posed to Kitty and been refused. It would be hard to say which subject and which feeling is primary here, as one usually can in a Jamesian novel, and indeed in most novels. Both the love and the land are matters of feeling—the Ryabinin episode is not merely brought in as a springboard to the private admission. The complexity of these scenes is not 'economical' and concentrated because Tolstoy is giving each aspect of Levin's life a fully realistic importance. The largeness and looseness of the treatment—not incompatible with a graduated movement to a climax—records a wide range of emotional reaction.

This is not the whole story. The life in this novel does not spring merely from a complex psychology which demands a complex rendering. In the scenes I have just mentioned, the character of Ryabinin flashes upon us briefly and vividly, but is no more fully rendered than many minor characters in Victorian novels. Apart from characters like Ryabinin, who have only a momentary appearance, there is a dense popu-lation of secondary characters whose life, from an economi-cal Jamesian standpoint, is extravagantly rendered. There is indeed something basically inappropriate about talking of Tolstoy's 'minor' characters. There is never, as far as I remember, any use of the theatrical technique such as we find even in characters like Mrs Poyser or Bartle Massey, who are given the weight of implied life and the vividness of personality, but largely by means of a sharp definition of idiosyncrasy, linguistic and otherwise. They are not grotesques, as they would be in a Dickens novel, but they stand in relation to Tolstoy's minor characters rather as the Dickensian minor grotesques (Mrs Micawber or Trabb's boy) stand in relation to them. Tolstoy's creation of this dense population of characters who have no grotesque definition and often no obvious function, whose lives impinge naturally and sporadically on the destinies of the main characters, is an essential part of his admirable freedom or what James calls his 'waste'.

I can here only briefly touch on this neglected subject of the population of novels. *Robinson Crusoe*, *Jane Eyre*, and *Wuthering Heights* are all novels with tiny populations, and the restriction seems to be an important aspect or function of their quality of dream with its concentrated selection of inner adventure. In Jane Austen the restriction has other implications, both moral and social. In Henry James the concentration on one or two centres of consciousness makes restriction essential, and in James Joyce economy and total relevance stamps most of his large population with structural symbolism. Even in the crowded life of *Middlemarch* the characters have, somewhere in their complex or lively appearances, a thematic stamp. There are no extras to give us the impression of either the bulkiness or the temporal flow of life. Indeed, George Eliot is occasionally given to creating shadows, like Gwendolen Harleth's half-sisters, whose names most critics would have to look up if they wanted to refer to them.

None of the novelists I have mentioned take pains to adapt the population of the novel to the flow of time. We do have occasional new characters appearing as time goes on, but we hardly ever leave any established characters behind. And vivid appearances tend always to be significant in the action, as well as developing or repeating the main moral preoccupations. In *Anna Karenina*, a novel much more compressed in time than *War and Peace*, some characters appear sporadically, some are left behind, and many have absolutely no influence on the main action. They are tethered to the action by their relations with the major characters but could be dropped without any loss to the moral clarity or even the development of character. What would be lost without such characters as Vronsky's friend, Yashvin, the rake and gambler and man of bad principles who is the only one who can understand Vronsky's passion and take it seriously? There is no obvious thematic contrast or parallel here, as there is with his other friend, Serpukhovsky, who emphasizes Vronsky's lack of professional energy and ambition, just as Sviyazhsky brings out Levin's vagueness and discontent, then his consistency and honesty. There are very many structural connections which give secondary characters in this novel the same kind of thematic function as in most novels. The difference is that the function is not invariably present. Functional characters are not only disguised by vividness, but may often only be 'functional' in the way they fill and complete a man's environment. We feel the real and full presence of Vronsky's life or Levin's because they are surrounded by a changing population of friends and acquaintances. Family relations are also shown in this sporadic way. Levin's two brothers have obvious functions of contrast. Nicholas brings him face to face with death, and creates a moral crisis which is not resolved until the end of the novel. Koznyshev is to Levin as Levin is to Nicholas, an apparently more determined and successful man. The family relations are presented with the ebb and flow of life, with contact forced by crisis and visit. Levin's relations with his sister-in-law, Lvova, and her husband, are beautifully and vividly rendered, though the relationship itself is briefly shown and the characters disappear from the novel very quickly.

Another striking difference between Tolstoy's realism and

that of the other novelists I have considered is his lack of contrivance. Just as there are no minor characters in *Anna Karenina*, so there are no coincidences or contrived encounters. There are only a few in *Middlemarch*, but it is relatively easy to move characters in and out and to contrive encounters in a restricted environment. In Tolstoy all the movements and meetings are brought about with utter naturalness. Not only are characters not brought together in contrived significant meeting by the novelist, but many of the meetings have no plot function whatsoever. Indeed, plot itself is another odd term to use of the novel. There is the story of infidelity in Dolly and Oblonsky, the story of the rough course of true love for Kitty and Levin, and the story of passion and death for Karenin, Anna, and Vronsky. But there is no plot in the sense of elaborate scheming and intricate intrigue. I am not referring to the absence of sensational discovery and coincidence and elaborate mystery— though these are plainly absent—but to the author's creation and solution of problems through plot-contrivance.

Nothing hangs by a thread in *Anna Karenina*. We may take for granted the way in which both George Eliot and Henry James hang destiny on threads. Supposing Dorothea had said 'Yes' to Casaubon on the morning of his death, before he went out into the garden? Supposing that Strether had not been looking at the river when Chad and Mme de Vionnet came by in their boat? These two examples are of rather different status. It could have totally transformed the novel had Dorothea given her pledge, as she intended, before Casaubon's death, whereas James might have devised a less coincidental 'discovery' of 'the lie in the affair'. But in each case, and in many more, George Eliot and James *contrive* their plot in this way. I am not denigrating their art by pointing this out (though I do, in fact, think the *Middlemarch* episode a weakness in the novel). There are very few novelists who even aim at complete realism, and we certainly tolerate conventions of plot which impose rather greater strain on credulity than either of these examples. But we do not meet with this kind of literary arbitrariness or contrivance in *Anna Karenina*. The plot has little responsibility for destiny. Destiny is the plot.

Not only are there no such crises of chance in the novel, but there are also very few crises of moral decision, comparable to those in George Eliot and Henry James. Their novels are propelled, for the most part, not by the 'mechanical' plot contrivances, but by moments of moral decision. There is Dorothea's decision to go back to Rosamond, Gwendolen's decision to marry Grandcourt, Merton Densher's bargain with Kate, and his last ultimatum, Strether's final renunciation. These crises determine the developmental structure of the novels, and they themselves are determined by the moral categories which George Eliot and James set up, and by the generalization which emerges from these categories. Tolstoy is conducting a rather different process of generalization.

In George Eliot and Henry James, for all the subtlety of their particulars, there is a basic sheep and goats division. George Eliot in *Middlemarch*, for instance, is applying a fundamental moral test—are the people acting from self-interest or from love? The novel raises the question, and it is not possible to answer it crudely, but by the end of the action we can give a fairly satisfactory answer, and never have to reply 'Don't know'. Casaubon and Rosamond and Bulstrode act from self-interest (and in one case, at least, this is not self-destructive) while Lydgate, Dorothea, and Caleb Garth act from love. Tolstoy is, I suggest, not directly concerned with this moral question which is centrally important in so many Victorian novels. He is more interested in a metaphysical question, in finding a meaning in a life so quickly ended by death. Even though this discovery of meaning frees Levin to love, Tolstoy's categories are not George Eliot's. His characters are not made to perform in the same kind of moral obstacle race.

They are shown as moving inevitably on their course, without being solicited by clear alternatives. Dorothea can marry or not, and when she does, she makes a grave mistake. So does Lydgate. So does Gwendolen. Maggie can choose to renounce Stephen or not, and when she does most readers accept the ethos of the novel and endorse her action. Secondary characters like Caleb Garth or even a major character like Grandcourt, are—exceptionally—shown without the process of choice and self-determinism, but the main interest of the novel depends on the movement through moral crisis and chosen alternatives. Tolstoy does not organize his action in this way. There is the implication of choice, of course, but it is given no emphasis. Anna could choose to renounce Vronsky, and, later, after Karenin's forgiveness, she could choose to stay with her husband, but we do not see her in conflict. We see her choosing unconsciously, with little debate. Her agony over leaving her son, for instance, does not come to the fore until after she has left him. Tolstoy is a marvellous recorder of this kind of drifting, where the uneventful moment, not the spotlit crisis of choice, determines the future. We see a slow accumulation of events, not a succession of moral crises.

A good example of this comes at the end of Anna's life, in the final quarrel which ends with her suicide. Vronsky comes in to find that she has packed, and they are both agreed about leaving for the country. Then he explains that there must be a day's delay before they leave since he has to see his mother. Anna uses this in order to attack him, and he gives in to her. She attacks again and forces him to go, sends him messages which do not reach him until it is too late, then sets off on her last journey. Tolstoy shows us these recoils and shifts in order to make it plain that the tension between these two people has become destructive—it is now too late for choice. There is no possibility of imagining alternatives, as there is in *Middlemarch*. If Fred Vincy had not listened to Farebrother after his moral lapse, if Farebrother had not spoken, if Lydgate had not gone back to see Rosamond in order to demonstrate his freedom, then the whole course of the novel could so easily have been different. The course of action which the characters reject is often just as 'likely', in terms of moral endowment, temperament, and social pressure, as the course they choose. The characters are placed in an action persistently punctuated and determined by decisive choice: the deeds determine destiny in a very literal sense, and the alternative determination makes its possibilities felt. Tolstoy gives us characters whose destinies are less plainly determined by actual choice, and where there is decision it is underplayed or strung out in time. The moment of choice is not isolated.

The dense vivid population, the slow drift of time, the unimportance of plot and moral crisis all combine to make this novel a much larger and looser form than *Middlemarch*. These features may also help to explain why a novel by Tolstoy is for some people difficult to read and for many difficult to remember. There is not the clear diagrammatic pattern of decisive incident and decisive moral crisis to create concentrated tension, or to act as a useful, if reductive, pattern in memory. Many of the vivid moments in *Anna Karenina* stand out as isolated in time, sometimes because they are indeed isolated, sometimes because they do not take place in a clearly patterned development. Take, for instance, the small episode, Tchekovian in mood and content, of Koznyshev's proposal to Varenka, which never comes off. This is actually an exception to Tolstoy's usual avoidance of the crisis of decision and the presentation of alternatives. Here is a moment of choice, and two possible alternatives. In the early chapters of Part VI, all the characters think of the likelihood that the match will come off, and in Chapter IV, we see Koznyshev weighing the pros and cons and coming to a decision. He will propose to Varenka. In the next chapter we actually begin with the words of his declaration of love, in direct speech, but when the inverted commas close we are told that the words are 'what Koznyshev said to himself'. He begins to talk to Varenka and she mentions her childhood, but then the conversation goes the wrong way, and becomes less personal. Instead of remaining silent Varenka goes back to their talk about finding mushrooms, and 'without wishing to' he goes on with the conversation. He repeats again the unspoken words of his intended proposal but does not say them aloud, instead he goes on talking about mushrooms. The banal and misleading conversation is a correlative not only for their inability to speak but also for their tension, but that soon drops, bringing to both the odd sense of relief that the words of the proposal will not be spoken.

Although at first sight this is very like the trembling crisis of decision we get when Lydgate goes back to Rosamond or when Grandcourt comes to propose to Gwendolen, it is in fact very different. Destiny does indeed here hang on a thread, but it is not the thread of social and moral pressures, but a more fragile thread of accidentality and triviality. No character in a novel by George Eliot has destiny determined by a missed cue, and although it might be argued that the importance of the missed cue depends on the lack of passionate urge in both people, we are not given enough evidence for such a view. Tolstoy is showing the importance of tiny threads. The unlikely pressures prove stronger than the obvious ones, and whether we put this down to an accidental lack of *rapport* or a fundamental lack of desire, it is presented as a movingly decisive accident.

As far as the novel is concerned, it is also movingly indecisive. The whole episode could be dropped without loss to the story of Kitty and Levin. It is true that it brings out Kitty's confident match-making. It also forms some contrast with the 'bite' of her love and Levin's, when she says to her husband of Varenka and Koznyshev 'Won't bite'. This local function is a small and subordinate aspect of the power and truth of the episode. What applies to the episode applies also to the characters who play their part in it. Varenka has certain obvious functions in the novel: she converts Kitty to an energetic charity which is both a help in breaking her *ennui* after Vronsky's failure to propose, and a moral false start which she comes to reject as wrong for her. In several ways Varenka acts as a contrast with Kitty: she too has had her tragic love (in the past) and she too expects a proposal and does not get it. We might argue that Kitty's character and situation are influenced and defined by Varenka. But the interest of the proposal which does not come off has, I think, very little to do with this kind of structural function. Varenka is as solidly presented, though in a brief space, as Kitty, and her scene with Koznyshev has an independent vitality. It is one of the moments of 'waste' in the novel which has its own incomplete life which adds to the density of the total impression. Levin and Kitty gain in reality from inhabiting a world of individuals, not a world of functional characters. The insistent function is appropriate to the moral exploration of Dickens or George Eliot, and to the dramatic economy of Henry James, but it is not needed in this novel.

I have suggested that this is a 'disposable' scene, but what I have said about the lack of developmental pattern in much of the novel applies to scenes which are essential parts of the progress of the main action. Tolstoy shows moral change as momentary and sporadic, not as part of a clear pattern of improvement or deterioration. Karenin rises to great heights of nobility when Anna's daughter is born, and he loves and forgives. Some time later his love and forgiveness have disappeared—partly because of the disappearance of emotional crisis, partly because of the influence of Lydia Ivanovna's possessiveness and religiosity. There is no straightforward line of development. A scene like the forgiveness of Vronsky by Karenin, in which everyone responds most nobly, would be followed, in a novel by Dickens or George Eliot, by a rising intonation of consistent progress.

Tolstoy's truthful refusal to categorize is seen most plainly in this instance, where conduct and feeling are shown as determined by the moment, and not as determining the whole of destiny. Karenin behaves plausibly but in a way which is unpurposive, unrelated to what goes before or to what comes after.

These cases could be paralleled by many others—Levin's reaction to his child, his combination of enchantment and disenchantment in the early days of his marriage, Vronsky's feeling that he loves Anna less, followed by his feeling that he has never loved her so much. These are part of the dense emotional complexity of the novel, with which it indeed begins when Oblonsky, the unfaithful husband whose wife has discovered all, wakes up, feeling happy and trying to hold on to his delightful dream about little decanters that were really women, then remembers that he is in a domestic crisis. This is immediately followed by the memory of his wife's discovery of the letter, to which he first reacted by smiling 'his usual kindly and therefore silly smile'. The psychological subtlety of the novel needs no documentation, and it is there in moments and minor characters as well as in the big scenes and main relationships.

In spite of its largeness and looseness, *Anna Karenina* is an organized novel. It has indeed many of the formal features of those novels with which I have been contrasting its plot and its populations. Its symbolism is never as extensive as that of Dickens and George Eliot, but it does exist. Its structure is less symmetrical than that of a novel by Henry James, but there is the movement of parallelism, contrast, anticipation and echo. Time drifts and is not always organized in crisis or decision, the moment may be vivid but isolated, but there is progress through a story—two stories —with shape and tension.

Like *Vanity Fair*, *Bleak House*, and *Middlemarch*, *Anna Karenina* is another novel of divided action. The movement from one story to another is itself a source of punctuation and emphasis, and the stories are meaningfully connected. It tells the story of three marriages, which can be roughly described as the *modus vivendi* of Dolly and Oblonsky, the tragic relationship of Karenin, Anna, and Vronsky, and the happier marriage of Levin and Kitty. This structural division is not nearly as plain as it is in the English novels I have just mentioned, because of the sheer density and detail and 'waste', but it does emerge as a statement of variations, significantly grouped. The characters inhabit a common environment, though the Oblonskys are based in Moscow, the Karenins in Petersburg, and the Levins mainly in the country. But the characters move about, from one city to another, and from city to country. One aspect of the contrast to which I can give no space, but which is obviously organized with care and point, is the value attached to various places, to Petersburg's ethos compared with Moscow's, to city as against country. And if we looked at a map of these significant places, it would have the conspicuous links of the railway. All this gives a representative impression of a large and varied society, with different conventions and codes and atmospheres, and establishes a firm sense of rooted life against which we come to ˙follow the rootless wanderings of Anna and Vronsky. There are family links, too. Oblonsky and Anna are brother and sister, Dolly and Kitty are sisters, and there is the added link of Oblonsky's friendship with Levin and with Vronsky. The pattern of these three connected actions is much less clearly balanced than the pattern of the four actions in *Middlemarch* which rotate in turn, each coming in for roughly the same proportion of narrative time and interest. *Middlemarch* begins with an introduction to Dorothea which looks as if it is to be the main story, but which takes its place with the other actions, linked by environment and accident. *Anna Karenina* begins with the Oblonsky family, plunging in at the moment of crisis when Dolly discovers her husband's infidelity, but the initial emphasis never repeats itself, and the Oblonsky story is really over before the two main actions begin. Dolly makes her decision, to compromise and pretend and make the best of things. Though she and Oblonsky play an important role throughout the novel, it is essentially a minor role, given its weight by their early prominence, but having no plot tension and occupying little space. For most of the novel we have a divided narrative, moving from the Karenins to the Levins, and each story has a tension which stretches from the very beginning of the novel, when we meet Levin and Anna in deceptively minor roles in the Oblonsky story, to the end, with Anna's suicide and Levin's vision.

This is an unusual construction for the multiple plot, but not I think, a casual one. George Eliot and Thackeray, Dickens and George Eliot, divide their narrative more evenly, whether the division is one of separate actions, closely or loosely connected, or one of separate actions narrated in sharply differing modes, as in Dickens or Trollope, giving us the equivalent in fiction of the main plot and sub-plot structure of drama. *Anna Karenina*'s uneven construction gives a free and wayward air to the novel, but this is not its only effect.

Tolstoy begins by establishing the normal case. The Oblonsky marriage represents the common problem with the common compromise: Oblonsky no longer finds his wife attractive, after several confinements, and both his sensuality and the conditions which give it scope, are established calmly, more or less taken for granted. The same applies to Dolly's acceptance and forgiveness: she knows that Oblonsky's repentance is merely a light punctuation mark, indicating no real change, and her love for him and for her children, her training and character, make compromise the natural thing. She minds very much but can do nothing. There is no need for further action—the crisis in the Oblonsky family soon ends, and the future is determined. This is the context in which we meet Anna and

Levin at the beginning of their more dramatic and varied histories, and Anna's passion and Levin's idealism are sharply dramatized, and stand out as exceptional cases. Anna, unlike Dolly, will not accept the conditions of her marriage; Levin, unlike Oblonsky, wants a stable love, and unlike Karenin, wants a loving stability. They are, it is true, more sharply contrasted with each other than with the Oblonskys, and here again the advantage of the chosen beginning shows itself. Tolstoy is basing his novel on an antithesis, the contrast between instability and stability, an unhappy marriage and love, and a happy married love, but it is not going to be a stark and complete antithesis. The first case makes it clear, from the beginning, that we are going to see variations on the theme of love and marriage, and not a rigid contrast between the Karenins and the Levins. Life is not going to be shown in terms of a grand polar tension, and the middle way sets up the right kind of expectations, as well as creating the impression of normality. Life is composed of Oblonskys as well as Annas and Levins, and this has a significance beyond the theme of marriage. Both Anna and Levin are people who make great demands of life, and although Anna's demands end in her nihilistic vision, and Levin's with his discovery of faith, they have much more in common with each other than with Oblonsky, the *homme moyen sensuel* whose demands are realistic and easy. Anna and Vronsky and Levin are all tempted to suicide—the difference between them and Oblonsky is most easily, if crudely, summed up in this fact. We cannot imagine Oblonsky's passions and ideas bringing him to this edge. His dinners, his work, his liberalism, his opera-girls, his wife, and his children, are all accommodated within his selfish but limited range of demands.

From the beginning of the novel Tolstoy sets up the antithesis, only to turn it into a parallel. He sets it up very quietly and gradually. The two actions begin together, with Levin and Vronsky as rivals for Kitty's love, and are first opposed only in this relationship of personal rivalry. The same applies to Anna and Kitty. Moreover, the antithesis is undeveloped for a very long time, until the second volume, when—at roughly the same time—Anna goes away with Vronsky, and Levin marries Kitty. Until this point we move from Anna's love-story to Levin or Kitty, leading their separated lives. Although, looking back, we may be conscious of the contrast between the self-absorbed passions of Anna and Vronsky, and the out-turned energies of Levin, this is not only a contrast which the author does not emphasize, but one which is not plain until the final antithetical action really starts.

Here the author does direct our attention to the structural relations between the two couples. We follow the first months of Vronsky's union with Anna, and the first months of Levin's with Kitty. But although the reader expects an antithesis, it is an incomplete one. Both couples are uneasy, tormented with jealousy, and Levin feels himself uprooted and without occupation, just like Vronsky. But in spite of this, there is the basic contrast between Levin's radiant joy and the restlessness of the Vronskys. This ironical offering of contrast and comparison goes on in detail. There is the contrast between the occupations of the two women: Kitty's conduct in Nicholas Levin's sickroom, and Anna's architecturally knowledgeable talk about the new hospital; Kitty's pregnancy and reactions to her child, and Anna's pregnancy, reactions to her daughter, and her subsequent decision to have no more children. Here the third term blurs the antithesis, for it is Dolly's point of view which governs our reaction to Anna, and in the marvellous scenes of Dolly's visit we have Anna's self-chosen sterility beautifully evaluated. Dolly has had her own private fantasy of having *her* Vronsky. Now her shabbiness and unhappiness make her see the glamour of Anna's existence, but she rejects it hastily. But Dolly's condition also justifies Anna—this is what happens if you stay with your husband and accept a

woman's lot. Finally, there is the contrast between jealousies: Levin's jealousy of Veslovsky and Vronsky's tolerance,
Kitty's dislike of his tone and Anna's 'civilized' response.
And at the close, Anna's despair and pessimism, generalized
in the last railway-ride, and Levin's qualified vision. She puts
out the candle, he sees a light. She sees the appropriately
peopled world of cheapness, shabbiness, and pretence; he
sees the endurance of the peasants. This too is a qualified
contrast: his vision is not going to be easy to live with, and
it cannot be shared with his wife. The very last page does
not set up unqualified triumph after despair—Anna has
killed herself, Vronsky goes off on the pointless Turkish
expedition, Oblonsky gets the appointment. Levin's vision
is set squarely in a realistic context.

Not only is the novel inconspicuously divided, not only
does it constantly compare as well as contrast, it cannot be
said to insist even on the pattern which does emerge. It is a
pattern which we may very well not be strongly aware of until
the end, when we may go back and see it embedded in action
which strikes us in its particularity rather than its resonance.
Levin's reaction to his child does not remind us of Karenin's,
both are striking in themselves. It is rather that all the
characters are subjected to similar tests, the common tests of
fatherhood, profession, and faith, and that the parallelism is
often scarcely noticeable. It may be argued that this is true
of most nineteenth-century fiction, where the pattern is the
means and not the end, and that it is only later fiction, where
the figure in the carpet is like a figure in a carpet, conspicuous and even an end in itself, that makes us go back and
abstract the muted figures of Victorian novels. There is, I
think, as much difference between Tolstoy and George Eliot
or Dickens as there is between James Joyce and George
Eliot and Dickens. We may not need to observe the structural relations in *Middlemarch* as we do in *Ulysses* or *The
Wild Palms* where we cannot read the novel without being
aware of reading form as notation, but once we start looking,

the relations are persistently present, governing scenes and characters and rhetoric. Sometimes it is very explicit, as with Dickens's extension of the prison symbol in *Little Dorrit*, so that the common symbol or metaphor forces us to see the parallel, and insistently. Sometimes it is less explicit, as in *Middlemarch*, where we can observe the difference between Dorothea and Rosamond without observing the careful contrast in the flowers associated with them, in their clothing, their attitude to jewels, their habits of looking into mirrors or out of windows. It is very likely that we may exaggerate the symbolic emphasis of such parallels, which are reinforcements of value rather than totally responsible vehicles. Tolstoy has relatively few symbolic reinforcements of this kind.

In *Anna Karenina* technical device never distorts character and action, by omission or stereotype, and seldom gives that heightened and poetic halo which cannot be appraised by realistic standards. When George Eliot makes Rosamond and Dorothea use exactly the same words, or when she makes Dorothea and Mrs Bulstrode perform a similar act of ritual in clothing, there is nothing unrealistic about the symbolism, but the characters and events are being artificially arranged for various purposes of moral and psychological emphasis. When Henry James makes Maggie find the golden bowl, or when Fanny Assingham smashes it, neither the plot contrivance nor the symbolic act are primarily moving as revelations of truths outside the novel, but are symbolic acts which have their meaning within the novel. We say of them that they are acceptable and exciting in that context, not allowing ourselves to judge contrivance or convention by the tests of likeliness so long as these tests are passed elsewhere, by the psychological detail or the moral generalization. When Dickens uses the motif of the wild waves in *Dombey and Son*, we do not apply quite the same test of internal reality, but we may again accept the convention as a poetic heightening, more or less successful in tone and function, which makes its first appearance within the natural context of character, as part of Paul's strained fancy, stimulated by his actual environment, and later becoming an unashamed piece of rhetoric spoken in the author's own voice, and not testable by reference to external truth. Neither the unrealistic contrivance which successfully pretends to be part of the imitation of the action, nor the unrealistic symbol, appears in Tolstoy. Tolstoy is of course contriving and organizing, but his contrivance is very muted.

There are symbols and recurrent metaphors in the novel, but their quality is subdued and literal. Take, for instance, the use of the railway train. This is not only striking in itself, and the nearest thing to a binding symbol in the novel, but it can usefully be compared with Dickens's use of the railway in *Dombey and Son*, where its association with death is powerfully exploited. Both novels deal with the expansion of railways, and there are many discussions in *Anna Karenina* which keep us aware of social function, novelty, and commercial exploitation. There are several significant railway scenes, the first scene when Anna arrives in Moscow, her return journey with Vronsky, the scene of her death, and the last scene when Oblonsky meets Vronsky. There is the railway game which Serezha plays, which has its grim anticipation. The railway carries characters across the map of Russia, and has the same documentary status as the buildings, hospitals, hotels, and farms. Only two or three of these scenes are linked by ironical resonance, and here the comparison with Dickens is interesting, because the railway is a monster for Dombey and for Carker, and never puts in an innocent appearance. Dickens does on occasion use the literal scene for such symbolic resonance, but not here. Tolstoy does use the railway symbolically, but in his own way.

We first meet Anna in Part i, Chapter xvii, at the Petersburg railway station in Moscow, where Oblonsky has come to meet her, and where he meets Vronsky, who has come to meet his mother, also from Petersburg. In the preceding chapter Oblonsky and Vronsky talk about the previous evening at the Shcherbatskys, and Oblonsky's cheerful bland impartiality links Vronsky with Levin, for he offers the same Pushkin quotation: 'Fiery steeds by "*something*" brands I can always recognize, Youths in love.' This first irony gives place to another, for Vronsky counters Oblonsky's mention of the 'lovely woman' he has come to meet with the same kind of banter, 'Dear me!' which is answered, '*Honi soi qui mal y pense*'. Throughout the next lines of dialogue Vronsky thinks of Karenin as some one stiff and dull. The train comes in slowly with a few accompanying details of 'workmen in sheepskin coats and felt boots crossing the curved railway lines', comment on the extreme cold, 'frosty mist' and 'frozen air', the description of the engine driver bent and covered with hoar-frost, and, lastly, with no emphasis, 'a peasant with a sack over his shoulder'. In the next chapter Vronsky sees Anna without knowing who she is, and we have the first impression of her vitality, as she 'deliberately tries to extinguish that light in her eyes'. Anna and the Countess Vronskya have taken to each other, and been talking about their sons, and the old Countess says to Anna, 'But please don't fret about your son, you can't expect never to be parted'. Earlier, in the middle of explaining how she has come to travel with Anna, she says to Vronsky 'And you I hear . . . *vous filez le parfait amour. Tant mieux, mon cher, tant mieux*'. He replies 'coldly'—in contrast to his reply to Oblonsky.

The brief scene is loaded with ironical anticipation, and acts just like a Jamesian scene, as the stage on which later action is to figure. All the roles and relations are to be reversed. By the time we reach the second railway-scene in which Anna appears, she is separated from her son, and the affection the Countess first feels for her has been replaced by hatred and jealousy. They are both separated from their sons, and on this journey Anna is pursuing Vronsky. On the first occasion Anna has come as peacemaker, to help reconcile the estranged couple, and later it is to be Oblonsky, with his old insouciance, making puns over dissolved marriages, who acts as mediator. All the characters are bound together, either actually or in insistent reference.

There is more than this carefully set stage, which is to be eventually upset. The railway is associated with death: 'A watchman, either tipsy or too much muffled up because of the severe frost, had not heard a train that was being shunted, and had been run over.' Vronsky's relationship with Anna begins: she only says 'Can nothing be done for her?' and Vronsky glances at her, goes off, and gives 200 roubles for the widow. Anna knows what this means, and when her brother asks her why she is so upset—as he has been himself a minute before—she says, 'It is a bad omen'. Oblonsky's '*Honi soit*' which was said so lightly, becomes a curse.

When we come to her last railway journey we see that Anna has learnt from the details ('cut in half', 'a very easy death', 'How is it that precautions are not taken?') when she methodically places herself on the line. The ominousness of original scene is not allowed to stay below the surface for the whole of this long novel. Tolstoy takes one tiny detail—the peasant with a bag—and uses him, just as George Eliot uses the dead face in *Daniel Deronda*, to haunt the novel, at very well-spaced intervals. Vronsky and Anna both dream of him. Their dreams coincide in time but in Vronsky's dream the peasant is a beater at the bear-hunting and Vronsky cannot see exactly what he is doing. Anna tells him in Part iv, Chapter iii, that she has 'dreamed it a long time ago'. The French words are 'incomprehensible' to Vronsky and repeated by Anna, '*Il faut le battre, le fer: le broyer, le pétrir*'. He is there at her death. The watchman and the peasant are oddly juxtaposed in the dream, since in fact neither Vronsky nor Anna have seen the first man. The ominousness is just picked up enough to provide the link of sinister recognition at the end. At the beginning, love and death are linked. It is a fatal meeting. And, a tiny but typical touch, we never know why the watchman was killed—he is the instructor, the first opportunity for the show of love, and the curse, but the refusal to tell keeps us within the observer's point of view, and insists on his stubborn opaque reality. The incomplete human detail shows life which is larger than symbolic function.

I do not think there are many examples of this kind of artifice and cluster, though there is the image of the candle, and there is the appropriate journey to death, with Anna's nightmarish distortion of her fellow-travellers. The symbolism overarches the novel, comes out strongly in these two crises, but is not part of the habitual mode of narrative. Even in these scenes there is the usual realistic stability of the women's conversation, Vronsky's reactions to his friend and then to his mother, Oblonsky's quick easy sentimental reactions. The scene ends 'And Oblonsky began his story', but it is Anna's which is really begun here.

The end of Anna's story is carefully related to the beginning—another reason, perhaps, why we feel so strongly the inevitability and lack of choice in the action—but it is also carefully related to Levin's story. Anna has crossed his path though they do not meet except once, late in the story, and it is Anna who has freed Kitty, and left her for Levin. She frees Kitty and Levin for their slowly-developing love, where for a long time obstacles from without and within hold up the development, and their love and hers are, at the end, contrasted. Anna's vision of 'anxieties, deceptions, grief, and evil' and Levin's final vision of faith and purpose are described in images of light. Throughout the last five chapters leading to Anna's suicide we have the image of the candle, which appears in actual form in Part VII, Chapter xxvi:

She lay in bed with open eyes, looking at the stucco cornice under the ceiling by the light of a single burnt-down candle, and at the shadow of the screen which fell on it, and she vividly imagined what he would feel when she was no more, when she was for him nothing but a memory. 'How could I say those cruel words to her?' he would say. 'How could I leave the room without saying anything? But now she is no more! She has gone from us for ever! She is there...' Suddenly the shadow of the screen began to move and spread over the whole of the cornice, the whole ceiling. Other shadows rushed toward it from another side; for an instant they rushed together, but then again they spread with renewed swiftness, flickered, and all was darkness. 'Death!' she thought. And such terror came upon her that it was long before she could realize where she was and with trembling hand could find the matches to light another candle in the place of the one that had burnt down and gone out.

Next morning she has her recurring nightmare (shared by Vronsky) about the 'old man with a tangled beard' who was 'leaning over some iron while muttering senseless words in French ... paying no attention to her but ... doing something dreadful to her with the iron'. Later that morning when Vronsky has gone out after a quarrel, the two images join: she asks 'Is it finished?', and in answer to that question, 'the impressions left by the darkness when her candle went out and by the terrible dream, merging into one, filled her heart with icy terror'. When she goes out her disordered mind sees its appropriate environment: Kitty's jealousy, boys buying dirty ice-cream, a tradesman crossing himself 'as if he were afraid of dropping something', cabmen swearing, lies and greed and hate everywhere.

There is constant movement: she goes to Dolly's, then back home to get Vronsky's telegram which has crossed with her note. She goes to the station, catching glimpses of 'the struggle for existence and hatred' which she sees as 'the only things that unite people'. She turns 'the bright light in which she saw everything' upon her relations with Vronsky, and sees what is true and what is not true. The image punctuates this vision of despair: 'the piercing light which now revealed to her the meaning of life and of human relations'. The things she sees in the immediate scene or in her memory are very sharply engraved: the complacent 'rosy-faced shop-assistant who was riding a hired horse', Vronsky's face as it was in their early days together, 'suggestive of a faithful setter's', Karenin with his 'mild dull, lifeless eyes, the blue veins of his white hands, his intonations, his cracking fingers'. The last train journey begins, and on the platform the vision continues to pierce, the ugly bold-faced young men, the misshapen woman in a bustle, the affected girl, and —at last—'a grimy, misshaped peasant in a cap from under which his touzled hair stuck out . . . stooping over the carriage wheels'. 'There is something familiar about that misshaped peasant,' she thought, remembers her dream, and almost leaves the train.

Her last companions are affected, insincere, weary of each other, 'and it was impossible not to hate such wretches'. She 'directs her searchlight upon them', seizes on the woman's words about reason being a means of escape, and asks, 'Why not put out the candle, if there is nothing more to look at? If everything is repulsive to look at?'

The candle and the nightmare come together again in the last words of her last chapter:

A little peasant muttering something was working at the rails. The candle, by the light of which she had been reading that book, filled with anxieties, deceptions, grief, and evil, flared up with a brighter light than before, lit up for her all that had before been dark, flickered, began to grow dim, and went out for ever. (Part VIII, ch. xxxi)

But the novel is not over. Anna made her first appearance, at the station where she first met Vronsky, in Chapter xviii, and after her death there are nineteen chapters to follow— fair symmetry for a large loose baggy monster. Tolstoy's artistry becomes very conspicuous towards the end of the novel, in this subtle interplay of image and symbol which we have just seen. The development of the imagery is part of the portrayal of character: its distorting flickering light becomes clear and piercing, Tolstoy peoples Anna's world with ordinary figures who can enact her nightmare, and the disordered sickness of her last hours is presented with poetic intensity which is the appropriate form. The contrast between the sick vision and Levin's affirmative faith concludes the novel.

It began with the drift of ordinary life and after Anna's tragedy comes a return to the normal flow. There is symmetry here, even in the detail, for we return to yet another railway journey and end, where we began, with the domestic scene. Part VIII opens with Koznyshev, a character we have not seen for some time, and there is an apparent diversion which tells us of the frustrating reception of his great book, into which has gone so much devotion and labour. With the typical natural movement of Tolstoy's narrative we encounter Vronsky's mother and then Vronsky himself, on his last desperate journey, which once more involves the individual destiny in the larger movements of history. From a Jamesian point of view, this transition involves a very substantial piece of intrusive action and feeling, but Tolstoy is evidently choosing to make an undramatic shift from Anna's death to Levin's life by using a character who is neither central nor deeply involved in the main action, but whose personal life has its hopes and losses too. There is the sense of continuity, a lowering of tension, loose ends tied up but not too neatly. Koznyshev is on his way to visit Levin.

Life turns into new channels. We move back to Levin and follow his climactic progress and the conversion to a sense of meaning and purpose. Like Anna he is tempted by suicide, unlike Anna, he turns away from the solicitations of reason and of despair. But this is no triumphant flourish in conclusion. The novel is at its most formal in this concluding antithesis. As far as one can judge from a translation, symbolism, rhetoric and structural relations are as pronounced and conspicuous here as they are in a novel by Henry James. And yet—in the very presence of such insistent repetition and balance—the novel is also at its most free and fluid. It is as if the frankly artistic contrivances are there to draw our attention to their own inadequacy. This seems to me one of the most important and interesting features of artifice and formal assertion in the expansive novel, and it is to be found in George Eliot and Meredith as well as Tolstoy. In Henry James and Virginia Woolf and E. M. Forster it seems roughly true to say that where the formal elements become most conspicuous, the human substance is at its most thin and sketchy. The reverse is true in Tolstoy and George Eliot, where a symbolic assertion of fable or category has the function of freeing the human material. The function of Mary Garland or Maria Gostrey is assertive at the expense of plausibility, whereas the functional relationship of Lydgate and Dorothea, or Anna and Levin, only makes the individual variations more apparent. The novelist's artifice may be held in tension with his 'love of each seized identity' or it may compete with it. The novelist's skeletal moral framework may show clearly in order to reveal the density and complexity of the flesh, or it may show itself by unfleshing identity. This is one reason for avoiding generalizations about novels and novelists and regarding always the individual form.

In Tolstoy the artifice and the moral fable show through more clearly at some points than at others: the loose bagginess may be apparent in places, tight organization at other places. The ends of novels are frequently places where a summary of value or an aesthetic completion will appear, and in the end of *Anna Karenina* there is a remarkable combination of the artifice which makes the moral categories absolutely plain, and the expansive life which resists facile conclusion. Candlelight distorts, and Anna's disgusted nihilistic vision finds perfect expression in the image of the candle, in its phenomenal aspect and in its actual nightmarish origin in her life. For Levin, light has a different source, larger and clearer in fact and associated not with despairing insomnia and drugged sleep but with great clarity. Its source is chiefly in the vision of the vault of the sky picked out by stars, but it comes too from other diffused images. In Chapter xi, which describes the sensation of converting faith we have the last moving description of peasants at work, and light and darkness are important terms in the scene which makes such an impression on Levin:

He looked now through the open doorway into which the bitter chaff-dust rushed and whirled, at the grass round the threshing-floor lit up by the hot sunshine and at the fresh straw that had just been brought out of the barn, now at the bright-headed and white-breasted swallows that flew in chirping beneath the roof and, flapping their wings, paused in the light of the doorway, and now at the people who bustled about in the dark and dusty barn; and he thought strange thoughts:

'Why is all this being done?' he wondered. 'Why am I standing here, obliging them to work? Why do they all make such efforts and try to show me their zeal? Why is my old friend Matrena toiling so (I doctored her after the fire, when she was struck by a girder)?' he thought, looking at a thin peasant woman who pushed the grain along with a rake, her dark sunburnt bare feet stepping with effort on the hard uneven barn floor. 'She recovered then, but today or tomorrow, or in ten years' time, they will bury her and nothing will be left of her, nor of that smart girl with the red skirt, who with such dexterous and delicate movements is beating the chaff from the ears. . . . What is it all for?'

There follows the brief description of actual routine—as in the hunting scenes, life goes on and man attends to work or play even in moments of grief or acute questioning. Then comes the brief mention of Daddy Plato, 'the upright old man' who 'lives for his soul and remembers God' and lovingly lets people off.

At the peasant's words about Plato living for his soul, rightly, in a godly way, dim but important thoughts crowded into his mind, as if breaking loose from some place where they had been locked up, and all rushing toward one goal, whirled in his head, dazzling them with their light.

The actual imagery of light continues, as it did for Anna, but more naturally, present in fairly obvious metaphors like the last one in the passage above, or associated with Levin's vision of space and 'high cloudless sky' which is both the limited rounded vault which his eyes can see, and the unseen 'limitless space'. It is the image of the sky rather than of mere light which corresponds to Anna's candle, and here the larger contrasts are more important than imagery. There is the pastoral contrast in his peasants and her townsfolk, his sky and her ceiling, in the sources of his stability—'the old beehives, every one familiar to him', for instance—and her rootless existence. There is his outward vision and her sick obsession. Both are presented in terms of clear sight, though Anna's disturbed mind clings to 'reason' while Levin tries to see his faith in the context of ordinary life where he will not be greatly changed, where his relationships will still be difficult, where no miraculous transformation scene will make everything different. But what Anna sees is not merely her own distorted vision, like Kay's in *The Snow Queen*, but the actual sickness and dirt and pretentions and competitiveness of the city. What Levin sees, more realistically, is again not his own blinding vision, but men at work, the stability and demands of the land and labour. What they see is what exists—at least in Tolstoy's belief—and, more important, it is what has made them what they are. This is perhaps why both are given light, and from appropriately different sources, manmade and Godmade, tiny and large, temporary and enduring.

There is no clear answer, and the very last appearance of the image of light blurs the antithesis between the two people, the two ways of life, the negative and positive vision. But this is only a blurring, not a disheartened questioning. The end is like the end of *Women in Love*, but more affirmative. It is like the last strong contrast between the mirror-gazing Rosamond and the far-seeing Dorothea, but less optimistic. It enacts Levin's realization that faith in life's meaning will not transform human relationships or break isolation. At the end he, like Anna, is alone, but his is a sane acceptance of the conditions of living.

In the last chapter of the novel, storm continues, and Levin looks at the lightning which does not illuminate:

> Levin listened to the rhythmical dripping of raindrops from the lime trees in the garden, and looked at a familiar triangular constellation and at the Milky Way which with its branches intersected it. At every flash of lightning not only the Milky Way but even the bright stars vanished; but immediately afterwards they reappeared in the same places, as if thrown there by some unerring hand.

Levin goes on questioning, feeling that solution is not yet discovered but is near, and he accepts both reason and its limitations, in a way which draws us back to Anna's last moments in contrast:

> 'Do I not know that it is not the stars that are moving?' he asked himself, looking at a bright planet that had already shifted its position by the top branch of a birch tree. 'But I, watching the movements of the stars, cannot picture to myself the rotation of the earth and I am right in saying that the stars move.'

Anna's sickness seems appropriately figured in the candle's distortions which she takes literally, Levin's sanity in his ability to entertain reason and faith, using the image of light and space with conscious detachment. He is joined by Kitty, who peers at his face in the starlight, and is able to see his calm and happy expression in a flash of lightning which also shows him her answering smile. 'She understands' he thinks, and feels that he can share his thoughts. Just as he is about to speak she begins:

> 'Oh, Kostya! Be good and go to the corner room and see how they have arranged things for Sergius Ivanich! I can't very well do it myself. Have they put in the new washstand?'

Levin is left to realize that there is no total illumination, no change, no communication, even though his life is now, for him, invested with a sense of purpose. His course and Anna's are opposites, divided in despair and faith, insecurity and stability, death and life. This final suggestion reminds us that human destinies are not quite so distinct. The pattern of the three marriages cannot be described as normal, tragic, and happy. The pattern of different energies cannot be described as normal, frustrated, and successful. Faith is not isolated and given a glorious climax, but brought into steady relationship with the difficulties of life. This is not only Tolstoy's admission of the free flow of life, made because he, like Lawrence, does not take the novel beyond the stage he had reached in actual experience. It is also an assertion of dogma in an undogmatic form, the last pulse of a slow and irregular rhythm which is a faithful record of the abrupt, the difficult, the inconclusive.

A Note on Certain Revisions in
Anna Karenina

MARTIN DODSWORTH

The draft material for *Anna Karenina*, edited by N. K. Gudzii, may be consulted in L. N. Tolstoi, *Polnoe Sobranie Sochinenii*, Vol. 20, Moscow, 1939. Fragment 185 is the draft for Part VII, Chapters xxiii–xxxi, the conclusion of the story of Anna. A comparison with the final version shows how Tolstoy reworked his first conceptions in the interests of heightened dramatic effect; this is done primarily, as Gudzii suggests, by giving less rational foundation for Anna's irritation with Vronsky, but the reworking of the episode of the candle is also interesting as evidence of Tolstoy's artistic aims.

Originally this incident came after the first version of the quarrel in Chapter xxiv, in which there is no mention either of the protegée Hannah or of Anna's 'unnatural' affection for her. Anna retires to bed and takes up a novel, whilst a voice within her broods on Vronsky's imagined infidelity: 'he loves another woman.' Suddenly she imagines that, though nothing about her is changed, she is back in Karenin's house, thinking, as she did there: 'Why didn't I die?' and at the same time wishing for Karenin's death: 'How often that thought came to her then, and how simple that wished-for death would have made everything.' Now it is Vronsky, not Karenin, who is the cause of her distress; but his death would only give her more pain.

. . . Taking off and putting on the ring on her fine white finger, she began to think: 'Then whose death is necessary now?' 'No one's,' she said to herself out loud, despite the fact that in her soul the question remained—whose death?

And again she took up the book and began to read and read, understanding what she read, despite the fact that in her soul, independently of her reading, the work was going on. She read that a woman had deceived her fiancé and he came to her. And here, suddenly, at the very same time, in her soul Anna's voice replied to the question: whose death? And the man and his fiancée in the book, and the window by which she had been standing—all that disappeared, and was replaced by a spluttering noise and then silence and darkness. The candle had burnt down, spluttered and suddenly gone out. Anna lay with open eyes in the darkness and understood what it was that the voice within had replied to her.

'Yes, the shame and ignominy felt by Aleksey Aleksandrovich and Serezha, and my unhappiness, and *his, his* suffering, yes, all is made right by my death. If I died, if my candle went out, then everything would be clear. But to die, to put out one's own candle.' She began to tremble from a physical fear of death. 'No, only to live, not to die, that's everything. I love him really, really he loves me. This is something that will pass.' Tears ran over her face, her mouth and neck. She quickly put on a dressing-gown and went to find him. He was fast asleep in his room. She kissed him on the forehead—bunching up his lips, he only shifted himself—and went back to her room. 'No, I get irritated without thinking,' she said to herself. 'There won't be any more of it. Tomorrow I'll make it up with him.' And she fell asleep with her mind at rest and quite forgetful of what it was that had set it at rest.

Tolstoy transposed this incident to the night preceding Anna's suicide, so that it clearly foreshadows her death, and the link with the last sentence of Chapter xxxi is closer than in the draft. ('The candle . . . flickered, began to grow dim, and went out forever.') He also radically changed the nature of the scene. Instead of lying in bed reading a novel (transformed in the last sentence of Chapter xxxi to 'that book filled with anxieties, deceptions, grief, and evil'), she lies drugged but with open eyes, watching the shadow cast from her single candle, and fantasizing on the effect that her death will have on Vronsky. The idea that her death will be a punishment to him and the attention paid to the candle are new elements in the passage. The novel which she was reading disappears in the final version because the thought of her death no longer seems connected with suppressed guilt on her part. By emphasizing the physical presence of the candle, Tolstoy surprises us with the symbolic import of its going out, just as Anna is surprised; on the other hand, there is no need for the crudity of 'to die, to put out one's own candle' (in the draft) because the mingling of Anna's fantasies with the play of shadows on the ceiling has prepared us for some kind of association between the candle's light and what is real and not shadowy. The candle's extinction recalls Anna to the reality of death, as opposed to her fantasies about it. This is vastly different from the draft, where it corresponds with the suggestion of her own death as an *answer* to her problems. Here it is what repels that answer.

There are important differences, too, in the handling of her visit to the sleeping Vronsky. 'She came up, and holding the light above him looked at him long.' What she sees is not only the genuine nature of her love for him, but also what stands in the way of its fulfilment, and that sends her back to the second dose of opium and the nightmare which, already in the draft, precedes the day of her death. Originally, as we have seen, she merely kissed Vronsky—there was no moment of looking and of vision; the candle had gone out. (Tolstoy had her re-light it at one point, and then cancelled the passage.) The difference is important, because there is another scene in the final version, absent from the draft, which offers a direct parallel to Anna's candle-light gazing at Vronsky—in the last chapter of the book, when Kitty gazes at Levin by the light of the stars and the lightning. The parallel is striking.

The association of light with Levin and Kitty is enriched if the reader is aware that *svet* ('light') also means 'world', 'society', presumably because these are what are illuminated. The contrast between Levin's large world and Anna's small one is therefore reinforced by the contrasted light imagery, especially as *svecha* ('candle') is a diminutive of *svet*.

In talking of light, Tolstoy, it is true, did not have much choice in employing a word derived from *svet*; his change from *uzh proyasnalo* ('Already it was clearing up . . .') to *nachinalo svetlet'* ('It was growing lighter . . .') in the final version of Part VIII, Chapter xvii, is therefore interesting. The introduction of the word *svetilo* ('luminary') into the final version of the last chapter is worth notice on similar grounds: 'the visible movement of the stars (*svetil*) round a stationary earth'.

A consideration of the treatment of Levin's 'illumination' in Part VIII, Chapter xi, is of a less doubtful value. In the finished text, it comes at the end of his conversation with the peasant, and the last word of the chapter is 'light'. '. . . Dim but important thoughts crowded into his mind, as if breaking loose from some place where they had been locked up, and all rushing to one goal, whirled in his head, dazzling him with their light': *vse stremyas' k odnoi tseli, zakruzhilis' v ego golove, osleplyaya ego svoim svetom*. Originally this moment came in the *middle* of the conversation, and was followed by the peasant's offer to lend Levin his horse. As the draft is not divided into chapters here, the moment could not be structurally emphatic as Tolstoy later made it. But it is striking that in revision Tolstoy altered the sentence describing Levin's illumination so as to end with the important word; he began by writing that 'everything suddenly came together to one thing and illuminated him': *vse vdrug soshlos' k odnomu i osvetilo ego*. In the final text of Part VII, Chapter xxvi, Tolstoy describes the moment of the candle's going out in this way: 'Other shadows rushed toward it [the shadow of the screen] from another side; for an instant they rushed together, but then again they spread with renewed swiftness, flickered, and all was darkness.' Having considered other examples of the use of light in this novel, the reader could reasonably assume an intended parallel between Anna's moment of darkness and Levin's moment of light.

INDEX

Note. This index is restricted to authors referred to by name or by work in the text. Bold type indicates substantial discussion.

Andersen, Hans, 209
Antonioni, Michelangelo, 27
Arnold, Matthew, 127
Austen, Jane, 2, 14, 45–6, 85, 137, 185

Balzac, Honoré de, 4
Beecher Stowe, Harriet, 16
Besant, Walter, 33
Bradbury, Malcolm, 30
Brontë, Charlotte, 1, 2, 6, 36, 51, 53, **61–74**, 80, 93–4, 105, 185
Brontë, Emily, 1, 185

Camus, Albert, 1
Carlyle, Thomas, 110
Cary, Joyce, 178–9
Chambers, Jessie, 140–1, 144
Chase, Richard, 70, 75
Chaucer, Geoffrey, 76
Christian, R. F., 175
Cozzens, James Gould, 4
Crews, Frederick, 75, 77–81

Daiches, David, 120
Defoe, Daniel, 6, 21, 36, 51, **53–65**, 69, 71–3, 80, 135, 185
Dickens, Charles, 1, 4, 11, 14–17, 31, 36, 49, 52, 55, 61, 88, 109–110, 126, 136–8, 185, 192–3, 195, 198–200
Donne, John, 104
Dostoievsky, Fëdor, 181
Dumas, Alexandre, 34

Duras, Marguerite, 1

Eliot, George, 2, 4–10, 11–18, 20–1, 31, 35–9, 52, 61, 67–9, 71, **106–31**, 135–7, 146–8, 168–169, 170, 172, 174–6, 182, 185, 187–95, 198–9, 202, 207, 209–210

Faulkner, William, 198
Forster, E. M., 8, 9, 36, 51, 53, **73–82**, 121–3, 130, 136, 180, 207
Freud, Sigmund, 140, 142, 145

Galsworthy, John, 132
Gissing, George, 121, 126–7
Golding, William, 81
Greene, Graham, 1, 81
Gudzii, N. K., **213–16**

Hagan, John, 109
Hardy, Thomas, 6–9, 24, 36, 47–48, 51, 53, **70–5**, 81–2, 109, 132, 135, 181

James, Henry, 3, 4–9, **11–50**, 51, 53, 57, 74, 76, 83–5, 101, 105–6, 116, 121, 127, 132, 146–8, 173, 183–5, 187–8, 192, 193, 199, 201, 206–7
James, William, 129
Johnson, Samuel, 172
Joyce, James, 2, 75–6, 132–5, 185, 198

Kafka, Franz, 1
Knight, G. Wilson, 163
Kotzebue, A. F. F. von, 14

Lawrence, D. H., 1–4, 8–9, 19, 32,
    34, 35, 49, 81–2, 106, 109, 110–
    111, 122–4, **132–73**, 174–81,
    209, 211
Leavis, F. R., 132, 149–50, 156
Linati, Carlo, 133, 173
Lukacs, Georg, 81

Maude, Louise and Aylmer, 175
Meredith, George, 61, 71, **83–104**,
    105, 122–3, 135, 146, 172, 207

Orwell, George, 53, 172
Owen, Elizabeth, 45

Proust, Marcel, 83

Richardson, Dorothy, 133
Richardson, Samuel, 81
Robbe-Grillet, Alain, 1, 2, 21, 25
Robson, W. W., 147

Schorer, Mark, 138–46
Sewell, Elizabeth, 7, 64
Shakespeare, William, 23, 37–8, 85,
    90, 164, 165, 166, 180
Smollett, Tobias, 61
Sparrow, John, 163
Stendhal, 105
Sterne, Laurence, 2
Stevenson, Robert Louis, 3, 32–3,
    34, 48, 173, 183

Thackeray, William Makepeace,
    147, 193, 195
Tillotson, Kathleen, 63, 68
Tolstoy, Leo, 2, 4–17, 20, 25, 32,
    35, 36–9, 49, 71–2, 106, 110,
    147, **174–216**
Trollope, Anthony, 4
Turgenev, Ivan S., 181

Watt, Ian, 54–5
Woolf, Virginia, 1, 7, 76–7, 207

Yonge, Charlotte Mary, 7, 64